VOGUE GUIDE TO
macramé

COLLINS – LONDON AND GLASGOW
IN ASSOCIATION WITH THE CONDÉ NAST PUBLICATIONS LTD.

First published, 1972

Published by COLLINS—LONDON & GLASGOW
in association with THE CONDÉ NAST PUBLICATIONS LTD
COPYRIGHT © 1972 THE CONDÉ NAST PUBLICATIONS LTD

ISBN 0 00 435084 7

Printed in Great Britain by Collins Clear-Type Press

Contents

Editor:
Judy Brittain

Technical Editor:
Joan Fisher

Editor Condé Nast Books:
Alex Kroll

Acknowledgements:
Drawings: Barbara Firth.
Photographers: Norman Eales –
Front cover, pages 4, 36, 40, 43,
46, 51, 52, 54, 57, 61. Richard
Imrey – page 58. Jo Swannell –
pages 66, 68. John Wingrove –
Back cover, pages 1, 74, 75, 76,
77, 79.
Still life photography: Maurice
Dunphy.
Hair on page 58 by Graham at
Vidal Sassoon.

Introduction

Macramé is the art of decorative knotting, and is immensely simple and easy to do, for no hooks, needles or other tools are involved, just your hands. Knots are tied in pre-cut lengths of string, cord, wool or other yarn; by arranging the knots in different sequences, an almost limitless number of attractive patterns can be created. Knots can be worked close together to give a dense fabric, or spaced out for an open-work lacy effect.

The craft dates back to the days of prehistory, for cavemen tied knots in long grasses and in plant and animal fibres, not only to hold things together but as a form of decoration. Through the centuries knotting as a decoration was developed until, in Renaissance Italy, it came into its own as a form of beautiful lace known as *punto a gropo* (knotted lace).

Mary, the London-born wife of William of Orange, is believed to have introduced the craft to England in the seventeenth century, and its popularity quickly spread. It was an ideal drawing-room pastime for candlelit evenings when the light was too poor for needlework.

During the Victorian era, the work—now known as macramé from an Arabic word *migramah*, meaning an embroidered veil—was used extensively to embellish the already ornate homes. Heavy knotted fringes and borders were made to edge mantelpieces and shelves, and even four-poster beds.

In time macramé faded from the scene along with all the other elaborate Victorian crafts, but now it is coming into favour again. Worked in the many exciting synthetic and natural yarns which are currently available, the craft has taken on an entirely new dimension and is being widely used to make fashion accessories and decorations for the home; it is also an art form in its own right.

The decorative aspects of macramé are shown in the wall-hanging and deckchair designed by Bo Ridley for architect Ian Goss

5

What you will need

Unlike most other handicrafts, macramé does not necessarily require special tools, equipment or accessories. In fact, perfectly acceptable work can be done with just a ball of ordinary string and your two hands. Because no hooks, needles or other gadgets are involved in the technique, there is no correct, or for that matter incorrect, method of holding your hands: all you are doing is to tie knots in a length of string or yarn, an action which you have probably been doing for most of your life, ever since you first learned to tie your own shoelaces in early childhood! Therefore you work in the manner which suits you best, and in which you are most comfortable.

Although the requirements of macramé in material terms are minimal (being yarn, and scissors for trimming), there are a number of dressmaking aids which will help to make your work easier. Pins can be used to anchor your work to a working base, and to control and regularise the shape, size and position of knots; they are virtually essential to good, neat macramé. A separate tape measure will be required for measuring yarn, and a large-eyed darning needle is useful if you intend to darn in loose ends at the back of your work.

You will sometimes find it difficult to work without a base on which to rest your knotting. In the Victorian era, when macramé was particularly popular, heavily weighted cushions were often used as working bases, and elaborate boards were manufactured with complicated screws, pegs and ridges to support the cords. Such complex devices however are quite unnecessary; all that is needed is a firm, fairly rigid surface of adequate size for the piece of knotting you are working on.

Any oddment of wood will do for this, but if the wood is too hard to take pins easily it should be padded with a sheet of foam rubber, or a layer of thick towelling, felt or candlewick. Alternatively, several sheets of cardboard or foam rubber bound together can be used. Fibreboard and cork can also make very good working surfaces.

It is helpful to have the surface of your board marked out in inch squares, and to glue a length of tape measure along the top edge, and down one side edge. This gives you a permanent, at-a-glance guide to measurements and proportions.

This board is an ideal base for smaller items especially if you want to carry your knotting around, to do on trains or buses, in the garden or on the beach, or while watching television. Bigger items however are not so portable, and you will probably prefer a more permanent working base. You can pin your work directly to an expanse of wall, or even to the back of an unpanelled door.

If you would rather not work on such a surface the knotting may be strung between two chairs, or any other upright supports; an artist's easel or music stand can provide good support, or a child's pegboard with the pegs arranged at suitable distances.

When you come to working in the round and on three-dimensional designs, a flat base cannot be used. A block of wood, cut to the approximate size and shape of the item you are making and padded with plastic or towelling, makes the best base, but it is easy to improvise here with upturned and padded pudding basins, flower vases and other similar everyday objects, to suit your particular work.

Yarn to use

String is the best yarn of all for macramé as it knots easily, holds its shape well, and the form of the actual knot is clearly and attractively visible. As string is available in different thicknesses, and also now in colours, there is plenty of variety to suit different designs.

However, any other type of yarn, natural or synthetic, may be used successfully, although you will find each displays different characteristics; some (the bulky ones) will get used up quickly in the knots, and so prove expensive; others (usually the synthetics) tend to be slippery and trying to control this can make knotting arduous. Sometimes of course the characteristic of a particular yarn can be put to good effect, depending on the final result required.

The best knotting yarns are the smooth cottons and linens, which are robust enough to hold the knotted shape: all thicknesses of piping cord are ideal, so are marine, household and gardening twines, nylon cords, dishcloth and string vest cotton, and upholstery threads.

Rug wool is also good, as it is more substantial than ordinary knitting wools and yarns. Knitting wools however can be used successfully, where colour and all-over texture are required rather than clearly-defined, crisp knots. Many of the novelty yarns currently available, such as gold and silver metallic threads and 'jewelled' yarns, also work well. They can be effectively combined with some of the smoother and more conventional yarns.

Macramé design by Kaffe Fassett

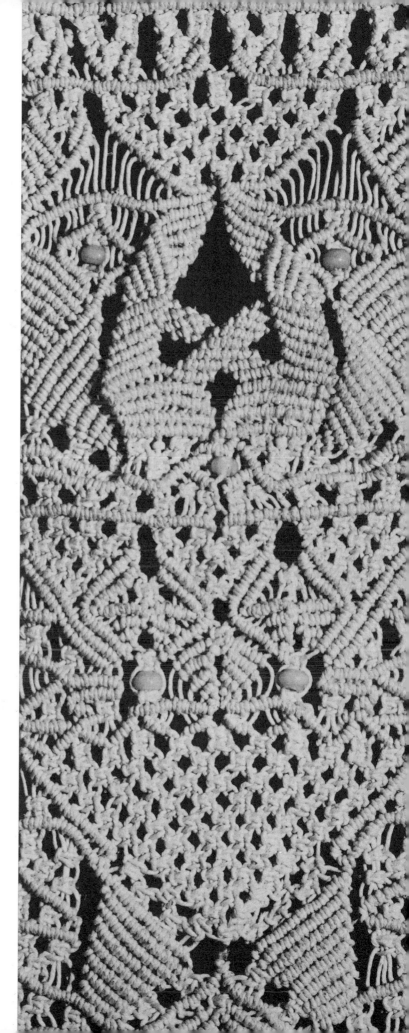

Setting on threads

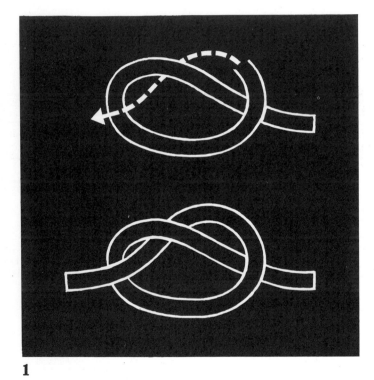

1

Before you can begin knotting, and this applies whether you are working on a simple flat sampler, a complicated design in the round, or a fringe for a fabric edge, your yarn must first be cut into suitable lengths to take them right through the proposed design, and then they must be mounted—or set on—either to another length of yarn, directly to a fabric edge (if you are making a fringe), or to a length of wooden rod or similar rigid surface.

One of the most difficult aspects of macramé is to estimate before you begin how long to cut each cord length. The tendency, especially when you first start knotting, is always to cut yarns too short—and as joining in mid-knotting can sometimes be tricky, not to say impossible, to under-estimate your requirements can be disastrous. On the other hand, it is a pity to over-estimate your needs, and thus waste valuable inches of expensive yarn.

As a very general guide, if yarn lengths are to be set on double (which is the usual method) then cut each length to eight times the required length of the finished piece. For example, if you are making a sampler to measure 6″ when complete, and you are setting on six cut cord lengths doubled, then cut each of the six cords to 48″ (6″ times 8). When they are doubled and set on, you should then have twelve working cord ends, each measuring a little under 24″.

To practise setting on threads, cut a length of string (or whatever yarn you are using for practise purposes) about 12″ long. Near one end tie

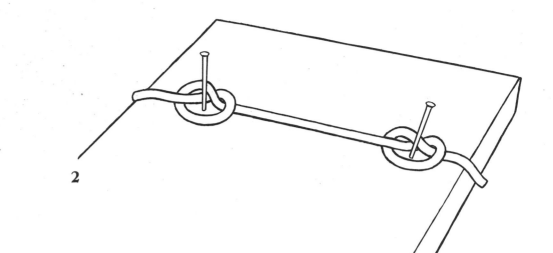

2

a knot by turning the yarn end back, then taking it up and round itself and through the loop formed. This is called an overhand knot (fig. 1).

Pin the cord to your working surface, taking the pin through the knot, then stretch the cord tautly across your working surface; tie a similar overhand knot at the other end and pin it in place. This cord is called a holding cord (fig. 2).

Now cut a number of lengths of yarn (as many as you wish to practise on). They should each be a minimum of 1 yard long. Take one length of yarn, double it and insert the looped end under the holding cord from top to bottom. Bring the yarn ends down over the holding cord and through the loop. Draw tight. This knot is known as the reversed double half hitch, and can be used, as you will see, decoratively as part of a pattern as well as functionally to set on threads (fig. 3).

Continue to set on the remaining cords in a similar way, pushing each set-on cord close to the previous one. There should be no spaces between cords on the holding cord. Now you are ready to begin the basic knots (fig. 4).

Note. *This method of setting on with reversed double half hitches also applies to setting threads directly on to fabric, or a wooden rod. In the case of setting on to fabric, however, it may be necessary to draw the yarn through the fabric with the aid of a crochet hook.*

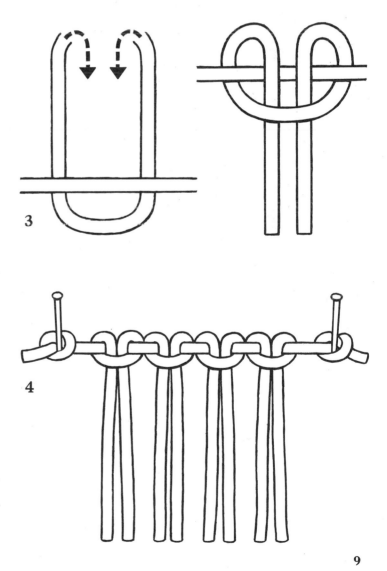

3

4

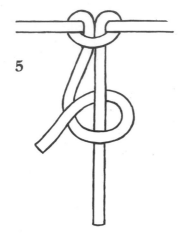

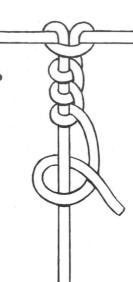

The basic knots

First basic knot: the half hitch

In almost every macramé knot you have a knotting cord (or sometimes cords) and a knot-bearing cord (or cords). This means that the actual tying and forming of the knot is carried out by the knotting cord, while the knotbearing cord merely acts as a support.

In its simplest form, the half hitch is tied with two cords only, and it can be tied from the right or from the left. To tie a half hitch from the left, the right-hand cord is the knotbearing cord. It must therefore be held taut while the left-hand knotting cord forms the knot round it.

Holding the right-hand cord taut in a vertical position, bring the left-hand cord across it, then up and round behind it and through the loop formed. This is one half hitch. Continue to tie half hitches from the left in this way to form a chain. You will find the chain has a natural tendency to twist around itself but if each knot is slackened slightly and eased as you work it, the chain should lie flat (fig. 5).

To tie a flat hitch from the right, the left-hand cord becomes the knotbearer, and must therefore be held taut. Bring the right-hand cord across it, then up and round behind it, and down through the loop formed. Continue in this way to tie a chain of half hitches from the right; again the knots must be gently eased if the chain is to lie flat (fig. 6).

An alternating half hitch chain is a pleasing and easy-to-tie chain, and used frequently in all forms of macramé designs, particularly for bag handles, belts, edgings, ties and as a form of fringing. To work this chain in its single form, use two cords and tie half hitches alternately from the left and right: i.e. for the first knot, the left-hand cord will be the knotting cord and the right-hand cord the knotbearer; in the second knot, the right-hand cord is the knotting cord, and the left-hand one the knotbearer—and so on (fig. 7).

A double alternate half hitch chain is worked

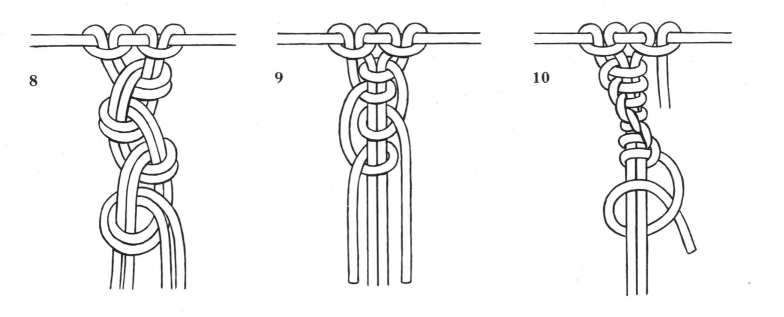

8   9   10

exactly as for the single version, above, but double thicknesses of cords are used throughout (fig. 8).

Alternate half hitches may be worked over a central knotbearing core of one or more cords. Try this simple variation, for instance, using four cords: tie a half hitch from the left with the first cord over the two central cords, then tie a half hitch from the right over the two central cords. Continue in this way, tying half hitches alternately from the left and right over the two central knotbearing cords. This forms a strong hardwearing braid which is again useful for bag handles (fig. 9).

Another simple but effective variation on the half hitch makes use of three cords. Tie half hitches continuously with the left-hand cord around the middle and right-hand knotbearing cords. This produces an attractive spiral (fig. 10).

Other variations on the half hitch are shown in the knot samples on pages 24 and 25.

Second basic knot: the flat knot

The flat knot is used in all types of macramé, in many different forms. It is a useful and versatile knot for it can be used to create a fabric—dense or open—as well as producing attractive patterns.

In its simplest form, the flat knot is tied with four cords: the two outer cords are the knotting cords; the two central cords the knotbearers. As in the half hitch, it is important to keep the knotbearers pulled taut all the time. In long chains of flat knots you can pin the knotbearing cords to the working surface so they are kept permanently taut; at other times it is possible merely to loop the central cords around the middle two fingers of your right or left hand (whichever is easier) and hold them taut as you work (this is not so difficult as it sounds). If you are working on a very large scale, or with excessively long cords, you can tuck the knotbearing cords into your waistband or belt, or even tie them round your waist.

The flat knot may be tied from the left or right.

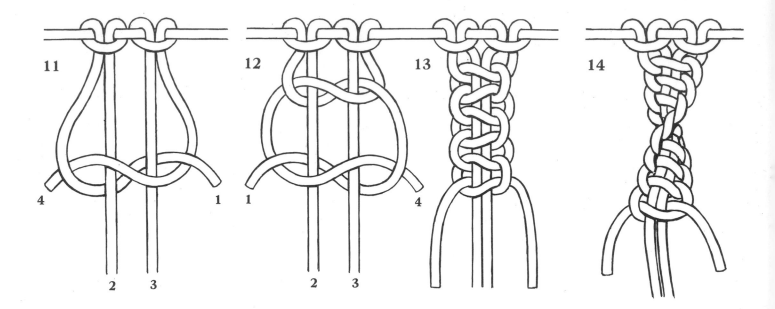

The basic knots

To tie it from the left, take cord 1 under cords 2 and 3 and over cord 4. Bring cord 4 over cords 3 and 2, and under cord 1. Pull gently into place. This is the first half of the flat knot, and is known as the half knot (fig. 11).

To complete the flat knot, bring cord 1 (which is now at the right of the knot) back under cords 3 and 2, and over 4 (at the left of the knot). Bring cord 4 over cords 2 and 3 and under cord 1. Draw knot gently into position. This is a complete flat knot, and cords are now back in their original positions (fig. 12). Continue to tie flat knots in this way to form a chain (fig. 13).

To tie a flat knot from the right, the procedure is merely reversed; cord 4 begins the knotting sequence by being taken under cords 3 and 2, and over 1. Cord 1 then is taken over 2 and 3, and under 4. The knot is completed by bringing cord 4 back under 2 and 3 and over 1, and cord 1 is taken over 3 and 2 and under 4.

If the half knot (first half of the flat knot) is tied

continuously, an interesting spiral is created. The spiral will twist right round on itself after every fourth knot. Allow it to do so, and continue tying half knots as before with the cords in their new positions (fig. 14).

A multi-end flat knot is simply a flat knot tied with several cords at once using more than four cords, and is useful for collecting cords together at the end of a design, or for creating a focal point in a motif where several cords meet. The knot may be tied with all the extra cords becoming knotbearers and only the two outside cords used to tie the knot; or several thicknesses of knotting cords may be used with a central knotbearing core of only two cords; or you can have multiple knotting cords, and multiple knotbearers, whichever suits the pattern you are working.

Other variations on the flat knot, including the alternate flat knot pattern, one of the most important in all macramé work, can be seen in the knot samples on pages 24, 25 and 26.

Cording

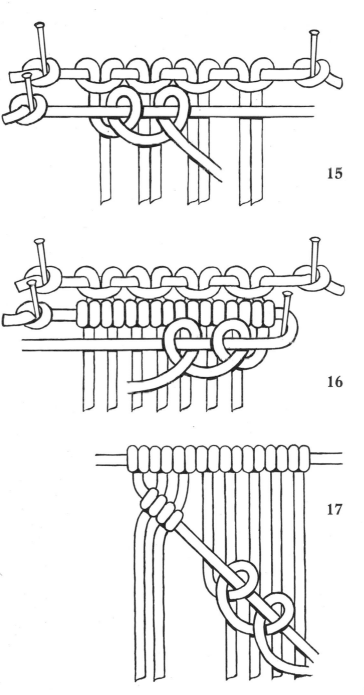

15

16

17

Cording is also a basic and very important knotting technique. It is based on the half hitch, and can be worked horizontally, vertically or diagonally, as wished. It is thus extremely versatile and can be used to shape edges, to control and regularise a design, and even to draw figures. It is also used in colour work to transfer colour from one part of a design to another.

In horizontal and diagonal cording the knot-bearing cord is called a leader, and its position controls the exact position in which the finished line of cording appears. The leader can be one of the set-on cords, or it can be a separate cord pinned to the side of the set-on cords. As with all knotbearing cords, it must be held taut while knots are tied round it.

To work horizontal cording from left to right, pin a separate leader to your working surface immediately to the left of the set-on cords, and stretch it tautly across them. If you wish, you can pin it to the working surface at the far side of the set-on cords to keep it taut. Now take the first set-on cord and bring it up and over the leader, then down behind it and through to the left of the loop it has just formed around the leader. Repeat this knotting sequence exactly, and you have tied one double half hitch, which is one complete cording knot. Continue in this way, tying a double half hitch with each set-on cord around the leader in turn. Push each little knot tight against the previous one (fig. 15).

To work a second row of horizontal cording (this will be from right to left), place a pin in the working surface at the end of the first row, and bring the leader around it; stretch it tautly across the set-on working cords as before, this time from right to left. Now work double half hitches over the leader with each set-on cord, beginning with the cord on the far right. In this case, each cord will be brought up and over the leader as before, but the end of the cord will be brought down and under the leader to the right of the loop formed round it (fig. 16).

The principle of diagonal cording is exactly the same as for horizontal cording, except that the leader cord is placed at an angle across the work,

Cording

according to the slant required for the finished cording. Double half hitches are worked over the leader with each set-on cord as before. You will find the areas of unworked cords above and below the diagonal cording tend to form curves. Pin these curves carefully as you work to keep them regular and evenly spaced. The leader for diagonal cording may again be either a separate cord or one of the set-on cords (fig. 17, page 13).

If you want to work diagonal cording from the centre outwards, select a set-on cord from the centre, and pin it at an appropriate angle across the work. Tie double half hitches over it as before with each of the set-on cords lying under it, working from the centre out (fig. 18).

Vertical cording differs from horizontal and diagonal cording in that the knots are tied throughout with the same cord. Usually this is a separate cord, but it may be one of the set-on cords, if wished, and each of the other cords in turn become knotbearers.

Pin a separate cord immediately to the left of the set-on cords. Take it under the first set-on cord, bring it back across from right to left, then up and under it from left to right. Repeat this sequence exactly and you have tied one vertical double half hitch, or one complete vertical cording knot. Continue in this way across the row of set-on cords, so each set-on cord in turn becomes a knotbearer. Always take the knotting cord under the knotbearer before beginning to tie the knot (fig. 19).

At the end of the row, the knotting cord is brought around a pin, then vertical cording is worked across the row from right to left. The first knot will therefore be tied by taking the knotting cord under the far right cord, bringing it across the knotbearer from left to right, then up and under that cord from right to left. Complete the vertical double half hitch (fig. 20), and repeat on each knotbearing vertical cord.

Vertical cording can, if wished, be worked on a single cord only but you must still tie knots in rows if the work is not to twist and become uneven; i.e. tie the first vertical double half hitch from left to right; tie the second from right to left, and so on. However, by the nature of this technique a rather untidy series of loops is produced down either side of the cording.

If you want to work vertical cording as a 'frame' for the edge of a design, it is better to work it on the two cords nearest the side edge rather than just one. The loops are much less in evidence this way.

Other variations on the cording technique can be seen in the knot samples on page 27.

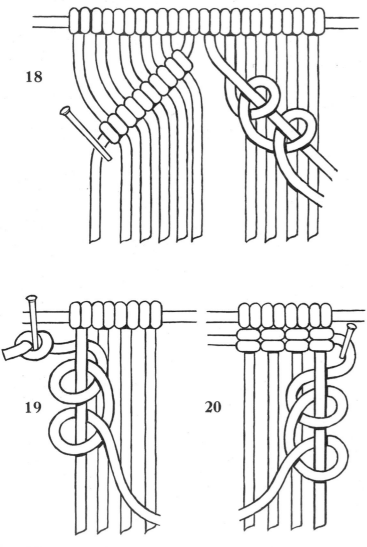

18

19 20

14

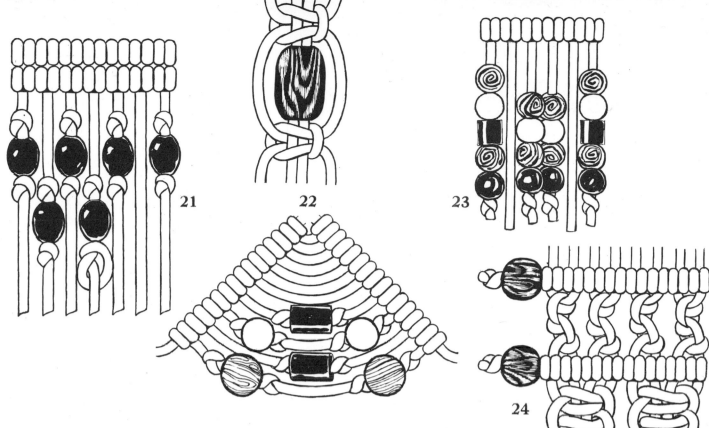

21 22 23 24

Using beads

Knotting may happily be combined with all kinds of beads, pearls, sequins, buttons and other haberdashery ornaments.

Beads can be threaded on to the cord ends after a knotting pattern is complete as a form of finishing or they may actually be incorporated into the knotting pattern itself, either haphazardly, in a free design, or regularly in a symmetrical arrangement, for example, as a focal point of a repeated diamond motif. Whichever way you may choose to use beads, it is usually best to tie simple overhand knots in the cord on which the bead is threaded, one knot above the bead, one knot below it, to hold it firmly in place (fig. 21).

The easiest way to bring beads into your knotting is merely to thread the central knotbearing cords of a flat knot sequence through the bead, after the half knot; it is held in place when the next knot is tied. However, beads may also be added to floating areas of unworked cords, perhaps in a cording pattern; or small beads may be added to the actual knotting cords (fig. 22).

Before you start work on a design using beads, it is best to plan exactly how many beads you will require and on which cords, then thread the required number on to each cord before you begin. Tie an overhand knot at the end of the cord to prevent the beads slipping off. Whenever a bead is required in the course of knotting, simply slide one up into position and secure either with an overhand knot, or by tying the next knot in the pattern (fig. 23).

If separate leader cords are used for rows of horizontal cording, an effective side decoration can be added to your work with beads. Simply slide a bead on to each end of every leader, push it gently close to the knotting, tie an overhand knot in the leader cord to secure it, and trim the ends (fig. 24).

Sometimes it is difficult, especially with thicker yarns, to thread the bead on to the yarn. The holes in wooden beads can be gently eased by working a drill through the centre; china or small wooden beads are best wired to the knotting at the place where you want the bead or pearl to appear. Take care to keep the wire hidden at the back of the work.

15

Multi-colour knotting

There are several ways in which macramé may be worked in two or more colours of yarn. The easiest method is merely to set on cords in different colours, arranging them in any sequence you wish, then proceed in the chosen knotting pattern. The colours will form their own pattern, depending on the knotting used.

To try this in its simplest form, set on a dozen cords, six in one colour, six in a contrasting colour, and arrange the colours alternately on a holding cord, so you have two working ends in the first colour, and two working ends in the contrasting colour alternately (fig. 25). Now work any of the flat knot samples shown on page 26.

This example demonstrates the simplest use of two-colour knotting. More complex patterns can be evolved by working in any form of cording. In fact, cording is probably the most flexible technique of all for producing fascinating colour effects. As the leader cord in horizontal, vertical or diagonal cording is hidden in the finished work, cording can be used to make a colour travel from one part of the work to another as though by magic. The contrast coloured cord is used as leader and when it is wished for the colour to appear, another cord is selected as leader, or else a different knotting pattern is worked.

As a simple demonstration of this, set on twelve cords, four in colour A, four in colour B, four in colour C. Now work in close rows of diagonal cording from left to right, slanting rows down to the right, and using the cord on the far left as leader for every row. At the end of each row the leader will drop down to become a knotting cord in the subsequent row. An attractive multi-coloured braid will be formed by working in this way (fig. 26).

Cavandoli work

This is a particularly effective form of knotting based on the cording colour principle as described above. In Victorian days the work was sometimes called wampum weaving because of its similarity in appearance to the wampum belts of the American Indians. But in the early part of the twentieth century a Madame Valentina Cavandoli, who ran an open-air school in Italy for young children, adopted the technique to amuse and occupy the children in her care, perfected it and gave it the name by which it is now

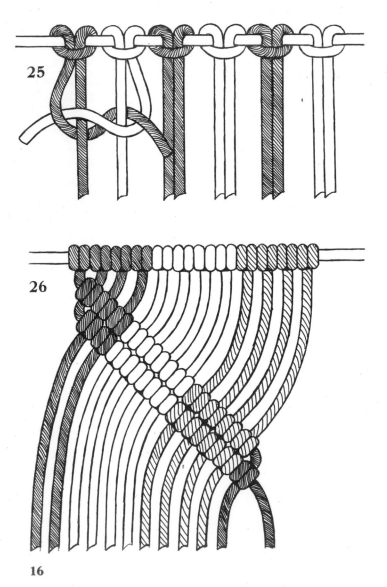

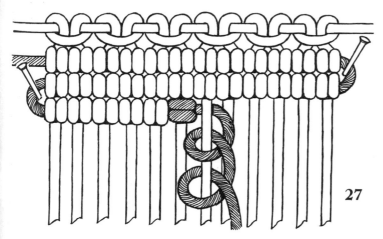

27

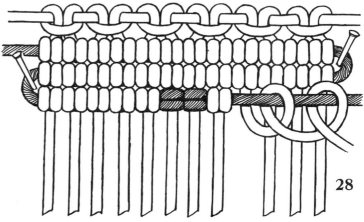

28

known. In fact much of her design experimenting was based on cross stitch work in embroidery.

The principle is simple: a number of cords in colour A (background colour) are set on to a holding cord. A separate leader in colour B (contrast colour) is then introduced. The knotting is worked entirely in close rows of horizontal and vertical cording: the background is worked in horizontal cording, a design is picked out in the contrast colour in vertical cording. The design is very often geometric in character, but can take the form of any sort of decorative motif. Normally a Cavandoli design is worked from a chart, each square on the chart representing one double half hitch (horizontal or vertical).

To practise the Cavandoli technique, set on six cords in colour A to a holding cord. Pin a leader cord in colour B to the left hand side of the work.

1st row (left to right): horizontal cording.

2nd row (right to left): horizontal cording.

Note. *Only colour A will show in finished knotting so far.*

3rd row (left to right): work horizontal cording on first five cords, then work vertical cording on next two cords, so colour B is now visible (fig. 27), and work horizontal cording on final five cords (fig. 28).

4th row (right to left): horizontal cording on first five cords, vertical cording on next two cords, horizontal cording on last five cords.

5th row (left to right): horizontal cording on three cords, vertical cording on six cords, horizontal cording on last three cords.

6th row (right to left): as 5th row.

Next 2 rows: as 3rd and 4th rows.

Next 2 rows: as 1st and 2nd rows.

You should now have a piece of closely-knotted fabric (not dissimilar to a woven fabric) with a clearly defined solid cross pattern in the centre worked in the contrast coloured yarn. It is possible to work Cavandoli knotting in solid blocks of contrast colour, as in this example, or by only outlining the design in the contrast colour, and filling in the centre with background colour. Diagram A shows the example just worked set out in chart form; diagram B shows how a similar motif could be worked in outline only, using seven cords (fourteen working ends).

It is possible to work an effective chequerboard pattern by the Cavandoli principle: alternating blocks of colour are worked in colour A (horizontal cording) and in colour B (vertical cording), as set out in diagram C.

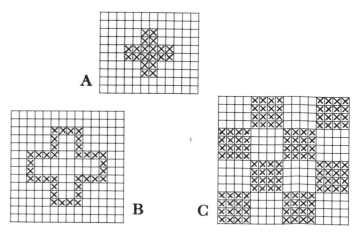

A

B   C

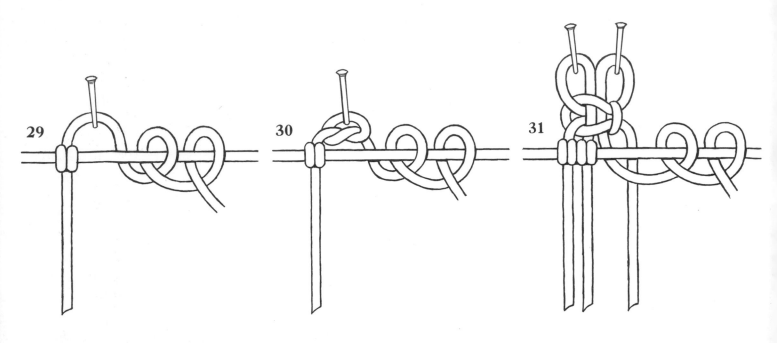

Starting and finishing

Starting

Cords set on to the holding cord with a decorative heading will add considerable attraction and interest to a particular design. The sketches and instructions below give a number of decorative beginnings, based mainly on simple picots and scallops.

Simple picot edging

Double each cord as usual for setting on, then pin it by its loop to your working surface. Lay the holding cord across the pinned cord just below the loop. Now work a double half hitch over the holding cord with each working cord in turn. The depth of the top loop will depend on the position in which you lay the holding cord. Continue to set on cords in this way so you produce a series of tiny top loops, with a row of horizontal cording below (fig. 29).

Overhand picot edging

Double each cord and tie an overhand knot at the midway point. Pin to the working surface through the overhand knot. Lay the holding cord horizontally just below the overhand knot, then work double half hitches over the holding cord with each cord in turn (fig. 30).

Flat knot picot edging

Take two lengths of yarn, double them and pin them by their loops side by side to the working surface. Now tie a flat knot with the four cord ends, allowing the loops at the top to extend fractionally above the knot. Lay the horizontal holding cord across immediately below the flat knot, and work double half hitches over it with each cord in turn (fig. 31).

If a greater depth of edging is required, work two or even three flat knots before laying the holding cord across.

Simple scalloped edging

Take two lengths of yarn, double them and pin them by the loops to the working surface, positioning one loop inside the other. Lay a horizontal holding cord across and work double half hitches over the holding cord with each cord in turn. The depth of the top loops depends entirely on where you position the holding cord (fig. 32).

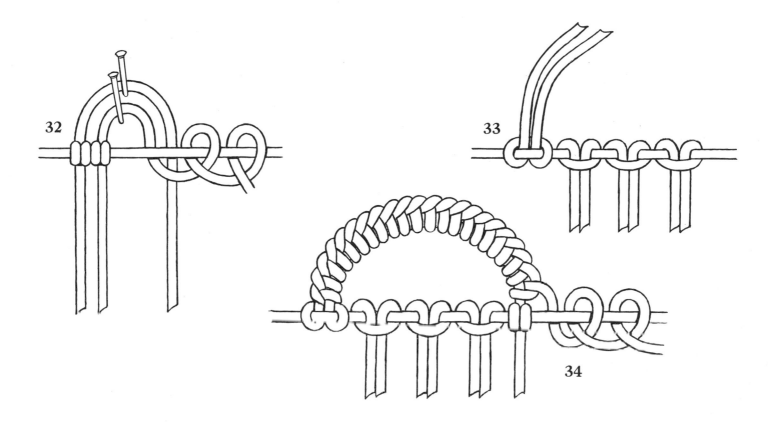

Half-hitch scalloped edging

Take four lengths of yarn. Double the first one
and set it on to a horizontal holding cord by the
usual setting on method, but in such a way that
the working ends are hanging in the opposite
direction from the work. Now set on the other
three threads in the normal way (fig. 33). Work
half hitches with the first two cords, knotting
cord 1 over cord 2 and gradually curving the
chain round as you work to form a deep arch
above the other three set-on cords. When the
chain reaches the holding cord with the desired
arch, attach the cords to the holding cord with
double half hitches (fig. 34). If preferred this
scalloped edging may be worked with a scallop
of alternate half hitches.

Finishing methods

Fringing. The simplest and often the most effective finish to a macramé design is a fringe. The
ends are merely trimmed evenly to the depth
required. The fringe may be left plain or may be
threaded with beads, each held in position by
overhand knots. If a knotted fringe is preferred,

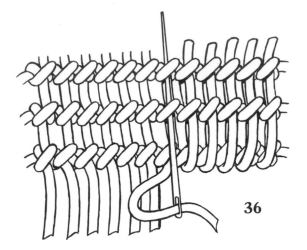

36

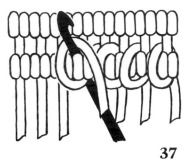

37

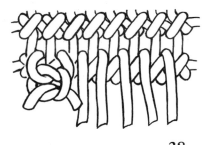

38

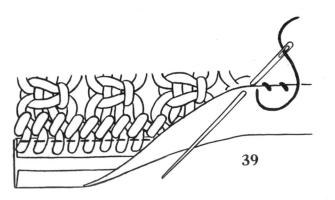

39

Starting and finishing

overhand knots can be tied either in single cords, or in pairs of cords together. Or pairs of cords can be tied in alternate half hitch chains. The particular form of fringe, whether plain, knotted or beaded, depends entirely on the design being worked and of course on personal preference (fig. 35, page 19).

Weaving in ends. If a straight edge is required at the end of work rather than a fringe, it is best to work a row of horizontal cording to complete the knotting; this gives a firm, strong edge. Ends should then be trimmed to a few inches from this last row of cording. Turn work to the wrong side, thread each cord on to a large-eyed darning needle, and carefully weave the end through the reverse of the knotting (fig. 36).

Alternatively, if two rows of horizontal cording are worked, ends can then be threaded from the front to the back of the work between the two rows using a crochet hook (fig. 37). Knot the ends together in pairs on the wrong side of the work in two-end flat knots (i.e. flat knots without the knotbearing central cords). Trim the ends close to the knot. If necessary, a tiny spot of glue can be put on the knot to prevent the ends coming undone (fig. 38).

Garments worked in macramé are often best finished on the wrong side with a strip of seam binding sewn neatly in place to conceal the loose ends (figs. 39, 40). Better still, if the garment is completely lined, all the ends can be sandwiched between knotting and lining.

40

Although macramé is more usually worked flat, pinned to a working board, wall or other flat surface, knotting can also be successfully worked 'in the round'. This is useful for any item where stitched seams are not wanted, such as a skirt, bag, hat or lampshade, and for three-dimensional sculptures and hangings.

Working in the round helps to ensure regularity of knotting. Sometimes if two sections of a design are knotted separately and then sewn together afterwards, the knotting does not always match exactly.

The technique of working in the round can also be used for flat circular items, such as table or medallion mats, or motifs, where work commences in the centre and comes outwards from this point. It may also be used for shaped items such as skull caps, tea cosies, and even lampshades. Alternatively, items can be worked in three-dimensional tubular form.

Taking the tubular technique first: simply, cords are set on to a circular holding cord and work progresses downwards in the normal way. A bag, for instance, can very easily be made in the round. A holding cord (which will form the top edge of the bag) is first cut and the required number of cords set on to this in the normal way. When all the cords are set on, unpin the holding cord from your working surface, and tie the ends of the holding cord together to form a circle. Adjust the knot until the circle is the size required for the top edge of bag. Now space out the set-on cords equally round the holding cord, positioning some over the knot in the holding cord (fig. 41).

Your normal flat working surface can, of course, no longer be used as a base. Instead a three-dimensional base should be used, as closely related to the size and shape of the finished article as possible. A piece of wood cut to the right size and shape for the item you are making is usually best, though for a hat, a wig-stand would be better. Alternatively, a pudding basin padded with foam rubber or towelling can be used, or an upturned flower vase (fig. 42). Knotting proceeds in the normal way, and you turn the work round as you knot. Slight shaping can be

Working in the round

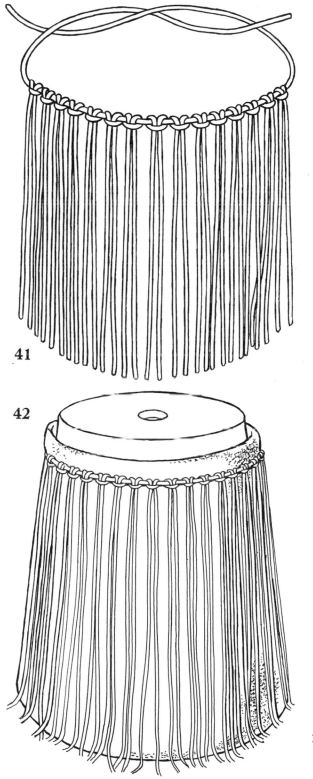

41

42

Working in the round

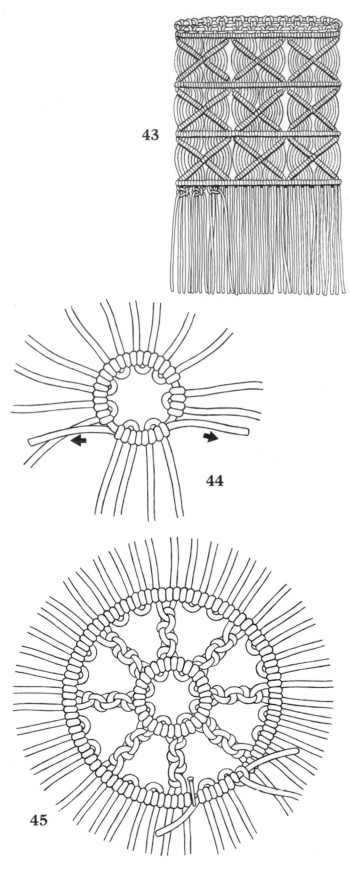

43

44

45

achieved by tying the knots in the first rounds fairly tightly, and then gradually slackening knots in subsequent rounds to increase the all-over width of the design.

If the knotted tube is to be left open, e.g. for a skirt, lampshade or collar, then knotting is finished by any of the methods used for flat work (the ends being either trimmed to a fringe, or turned in and woven into the wrong side of the last few rows of knotting). However, if it is wished to close the tube, as, for instance, for a bag, then the edges may either be sewn or knotted together. Remove the work from the three-dimensional base, and lay it on a flat base, so the work lies in the form of a finished bag. Now work knots across the lower edge, combining cords from the front with cords from the back in every knot (fig. 43). Trim the ends to a fringe of the required depth, or add tassels.

In articles to be flat in finished form, but worked in the round (e.g. a circular table mat), start from a central point and work outwards, using your normal flat working surface.

The basic method of starting work is the same for a flat or shaped item. Cords may be set on to a holding cord or directly on to a metal, plastic or wooden ring. If setting on to a holding cord, set on just a few cords first, then overlap the ends of the holding cord, and set on a few more cords over this double thickness. Pull the ends of the holding cord to tighten to the desired size, then space out the set-on cords equally round it, adding more if required (fig. 44).

Now work knots in the chosen pattern. Unless you are using a very open-work pattern, extra cords will have to be added as the circle gradually enlarges. The easiest way to do this is to work rows of cording at intervals and introduce the new cords into these (fig. 45).

Washing and dyeing

As with knitwear, or any other fabric, items made from macramé need careful handling and regular cleaning if they are to stay looking their best. The basic rules of laundering for different fibres, both natural and man-made, apply equally to macramé. Very heavy items, however, are best dry-cleaned, as their weight when wet could pull a design out of shape, or distort the knots. The following is a brief guide to washing different fibre types.

Cottons and linens (including ordinary string)
Add mild detergent or soap flakes to hot water. Whip up to a good lather then add cold water to reduce the temperature to hand-hot. Place macramé items in this soapy solution. Squeeze gently to remove dirt, never rub or twist. Rinse well, and leave to dry on a flat surface. A mild solution of starch dabbed over the article before you press it will give a slight stiffening.

All weights of wools
Wash very gently in lukewarm soapy water. Rinse well, at least three times. If the third rinse is still not crystal clear, then rinse again. Gently squeeze the item after the final rinse, and roll it in a clean dry white towel. Do not twist. Spread the item to dry on a flat surface, eased into its correct shape and size. Leave to dry away from direct heat or sunlight. If pressing is required, do so carefully on the wrong side of the item, with a moderate iron over a damp cloth.

Synthetics
Wash as for wool. No pressing should be required. Plastic-coated strings, polypropylene, and other similar synthetic cords need only an occasional wipe over with a soapy cloth to keep them clean.

Piping cords
Wash as for cottons. Items made in heavy piping cords should always be dry-cleaned.

Dyeing
Most macramé yarns may be successfully home dyed, thus giving a wider range of colours than would otherwise be possible. Strings dye particularly well and so do piping cords. There are many excellent proprietary brands of dyes on the market, to suit different yarns and different purposes; choose the dye to suit your material.

Yarn may either be dyed in its loose state, or after being made up into a garment or other item. If dyeing yarn in its loose state, wind it into big loose coils, then tie it together with small pieces of fine thread. Move the yarn about during the dyeing period with a wooden spoon. This will allow the dye solution to coat the surface of the yarn evenly.

Whichever type of dye you use, and whatever yarn, it is important to dye a sufficient quantity for your requirements all at once. Always overestimate your needs, as a secondary dyeing with a different dye solution rarely yields exactly the same depth of colour as the first.

The following is a basic guide to dye types:
Cold dyes: colour and light fast, many brilliant colours. Good for all natural fibres.
Wash and dye dyes: for washing-machine dyeing of large items. Suitable for natural fibres and nylons, but not polyesters, acrylics, or yarns with special finishes.
Instant liquid dyes: simple, easy and quick to use. Just add a measure of dye solution straight from the bottle to hot water. For all washable fabrics, except acrylics.
Multi-purpose dyes and tints: range of excellent colours. Suitable for all natural and most synthetic fibres.

Free service for home dyers
If you are in any doubt at all about which type of dye to use for a particular yarn, send a small sample of the yarn to Annette Stevens at the Consumer Advice Bureau, Dylon International Ltd., Lower Sydenham, London SE26 5HO.

Knot samples

Half hitch variations

SAMPLE A
Worked on four cords. *Work half hitches from the left with cord 1, first over cord 2, then over cords 2 and 3 together, then over cord 2; work half hitches from the right with cord 4, first over cord 3, then over cords 3 and 2 together, then over cord 3.** Repeat from * to ** for the length required.

SAMPLE B
Worked on four cords. * Work five half hitches from the left with cord 1 over cords 2 and 3, then work five half hitches from the right with cord 4 over cords 3 and 2.** Repeat from * to ** to the length required. This is a waved bar.

SAMPLE C
Worked on four cords. Work a half hitch from the left with cord 1 over cords 2 and 3. Work a second half hitch from the left with cord 1 over 2 and 3, but work the knot in reverse—i.e. take it first *under* the knotbearing cords, then bring it over them from right to left, and down through the loop formed. Draw tight. The complete knot is known as the reversed double half hitch. In a similar way, work a reversed double half hitch from the right with cord 4 over cords 3 and 2. Continue to work reversed double half hitches from the left and right alternately to the length required.

Flat knot variations

SAMPLE D
Worked on four cords. Tie a flat knot followed by the first half of a flat knot, i.e. you will have tied 1½ flat knots (this is a triple knot). Now on the central knotbearing cords tie an overhand knot. Bring the outer (knotting) cords down on either side of the overhand knot and tie another triple knot immediately below the overhand knot, with all cords. Continue in this way alternately tying overhand knots and triple knots to the length required.

A

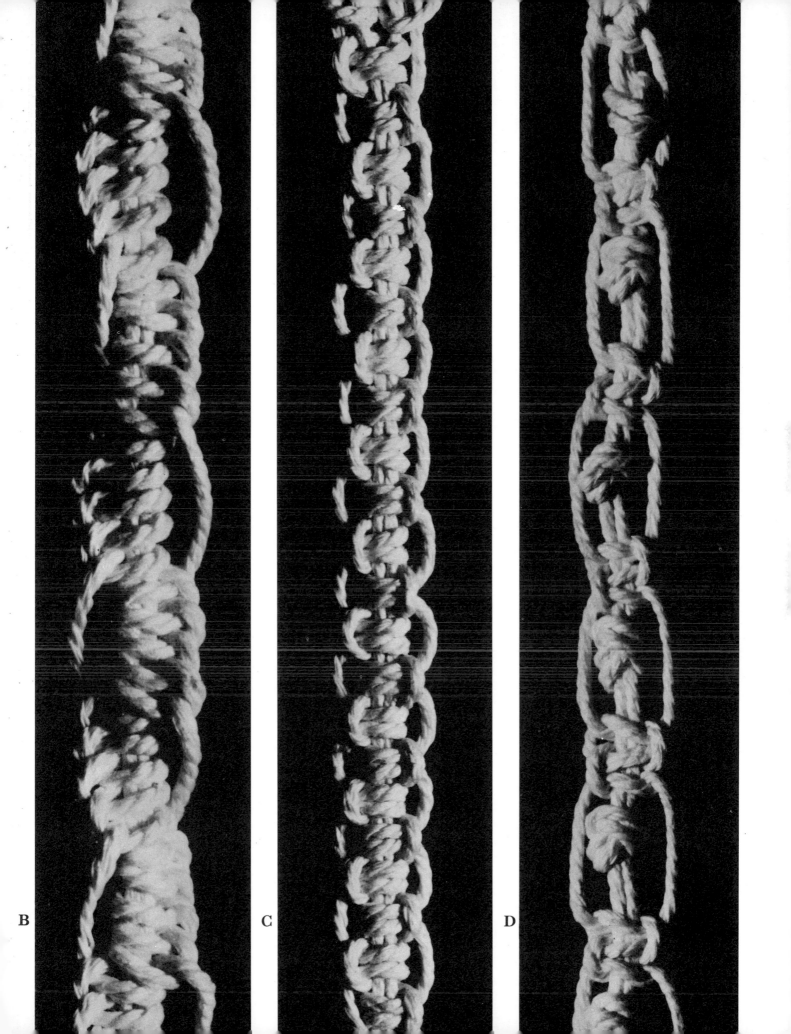

B   C   D

E

F

Knot samples

SAMPLE E
This is the alternate flat knot pattern which occurs frequently in all types of macramé work. Set on cords in any multiple of four.

1st row: tie four-end flat knots with each group of four cords to the end of the row.
2nd row: leave the first two cords unworked; tie flat knots with each group of four cords to the last two cords; leave these last two cords unworked.
3rd row: as first row.
4th row: as second row.
Continue in this way. If the knots are pulled tightly together a dense fabric will be produced; if they are spaced out evenly a lacy pattern will be made.

SAMPLE F
A variation on the alternate flat knot pattern. Set on cords in multiples of four. Work as for Sample E, but work chains of three flat knots each time instead of single knots.

SAMPLE G
Another variation on the alternate flat knot pattern. Set on cords in multiples of four.

*1st row: work three flat knots with each group of four cords to the end of the row.
Next row: leave the first two cords unworked; tie single flat knots with each group of four cords to the last two cords; leave these two cords unworked.
Next row: work single flat knots with each group of four cords to the end of the row.
Next row: leave the first two cords unworked; tie three flat knots with each group of four cords to the last two cords; leave these last two cords unworked.
Next row: tie single flat knots with each group of four cords to the end of the row.
Next row: leave the first two cords unworked.******
Repeat from * to ** to the length required.

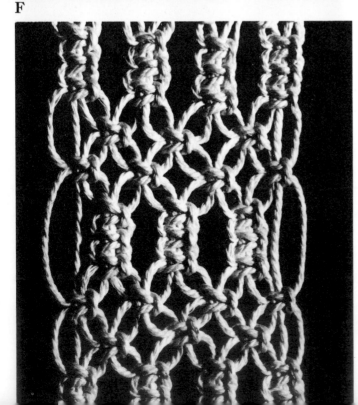

G

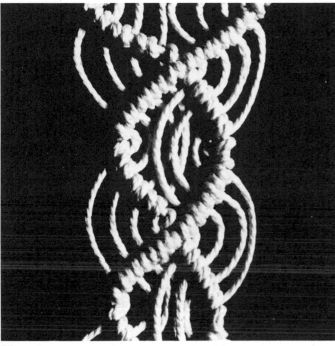

H

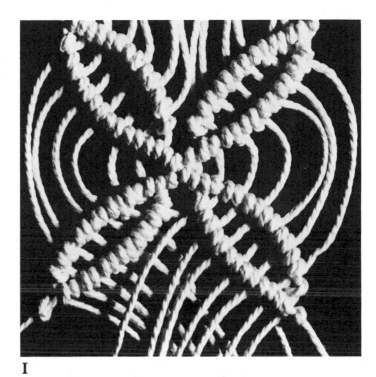

I

Cording variations

SAMPLE H

Worked on 10 cords. With cord 1 as leader, work diagonal cording slanting down to the right with cords 2, 3, 4 and 5. With cord 10 as leader, work diagonal cording slanting down to the left with cords 9, 8, 7 and 6. Link the two leaders by working cording with cord 1 over cord 10. Cord 10 now continues as leader across the work at the same slant as before. Work diagonal cording over it with cords 5, 4, 3 and 2.

Cord 1 continues as leader across the other side of the work, and diagonal cording slanting down to the right is worked over it with cords 6, 7, 8 and 9.

Reverse the direction of cord 10 round a pin and let it continue as leader slanting down to the right. Work cording over it with cords 2, 3, 4 and 5. Similarly reverse the direction of cord 1 round a pin, and work cording slanting down to the left over it with cords 9, 8, 7 and 6. Link the two leaders by knotting cord 10 over cord 1. Continue in this way to form diamonds of cording.

SAMPLE I

A four-leaf cording motif worked on 16 cords. Work the top left-hand leaf first: with cord 1 as leader, pin it in position to form the upper curve of a leaf. Work cording over it with cords 2, 3, 4, 5, 6, 7 and 8. With cord 2 as leader, pin it in position to form the lower curve of a leaf. Work cording over it with cords, 3, 4, 5, 6, 7, 8 and 1. In a similar way work the top right-hand leaf. This time cord 16 will be leader for the top curve of the leaf, and cording will be worked from right to left. Cord 15 will be the leader for the lower curve of the leaf.

Link the lower corners of the two leaves just worked by knotting cord 15 over cord 2.

Now work the lower left-hand leaf. Cord 15 continues across the work as leader for the top curve of the leaf, and cording is worked over it from right to left with cords 1, 8, 7, 6, 5, 4 and 3. Cord 1 then becomes leader for the lower curve of the leaf and cords 8, 7, 6, 5, 4, 3 and 15 are knotted over it.

Complete the motif with the lower right-hand leaf: cord 2 continues across the work as leader for the top curve of the leaf, cording worked over it from left to right. Finally cord 16 is leader for the lower curve of this leaf.

Braids

A 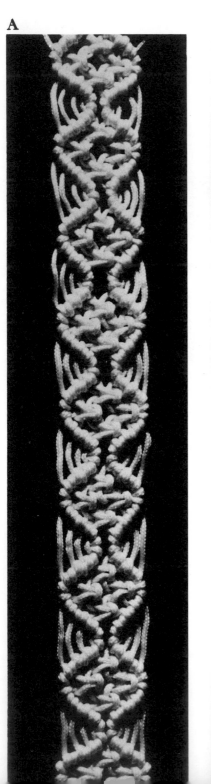 B

BRAID A

MATERIAL. Fine nylon cord.
NUMBER OF CORDS. Ten.
TO MAKE

With cord 5 as leader, work diagonal cording slanting down to the left with cords 4, 3, 2 and 1. In a similar way work diagonal cording slanting down to the right using cord 6 as leader, and knotting cords 7, 8, 9 and 10 over it.

Now tie a flat knot in the centre with cords 3, 4, 7 and 8.

Next row: tie a flat knot with cords 1, 2, 3 and 4, and another flat knot with cords 7, 8, 9 and 10.

Next row: tie a flat knot with cords 3, 4, 7 and 8. Continuing to use cord 5 as leader, reverse its direction round a pin and work diagonal cording slanting to the right with cords 1, 2, 3 and 4. Similarly work diagonal cording slanting to the left with cords 10, 9, 8 and 7 over cord 6. Reverse the direction of the leaders round pins and repeat the motif, allowing unworked areas of cords at the sides (between motifs) to form gentle and regular curves. Continue in this way until braid is the desired length.

BRAID B

MATERIAL. Medium nylon cord.
NUMBER OF CORDS. Four.
TO MAKE

Work flat knots at 1½" intervals. After each knot is tied, cross cord 2 over 1, and 3 over 4, so the knotting cords of the previous knot become the knotbearers in the following knot.

BRAID C

MATERIAL. Rug wool in two contrasting shades.
NUMBER OF CORDS. Six, arranged in the following colour sequence: three cords in colour A, two in colour B, and one in colour A.

TO MAKE

Tie flat knots at 1″ intervals, using only the two outer cords as knotting cords, i.e. the knotbearing core will consist of two cords in colour A, two in colour B. Let the knotting cords form regular loops (picots) at either side of the braid.

BRAID D

MATERIAL. Piping cord No. 1.
NUMBER OF CORDS. Eight.

TO MAKE

*Knot a reversed double half hitch from left to right with cord 1 over cords 2 and 3; take cord 5 under cord 4 and use it to tie a reversed double half hitch from right to left over cords 2 and 3. Now tie a reversed double half hitch from right to left with cord 8 over cords 6 and 7, then tie a reversed double half hitch from left to right with cord 4 over 6 and 7.

Tie a reversed double half hitch from left to right with cord 1 over cords 2 and 3, bring cord 4 under cord 5 and use it to tie a reversed double half hitch from right to left over cords 2 and 3. Tie a reversed double half hitch from right to left with cord 8 over cords 6 and 7; tie a reversed double half hitch from left to right with cord 5 over cords 6 and 7.** Repeat from * to ** until braid is the required length.

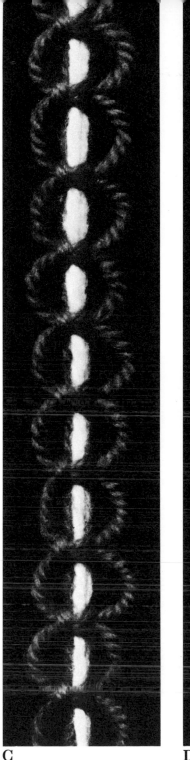

C

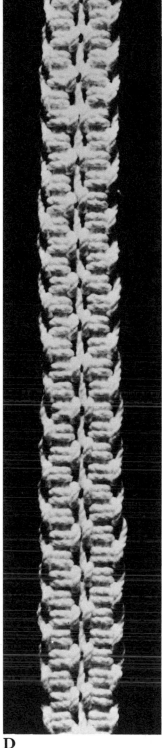

D

Braids

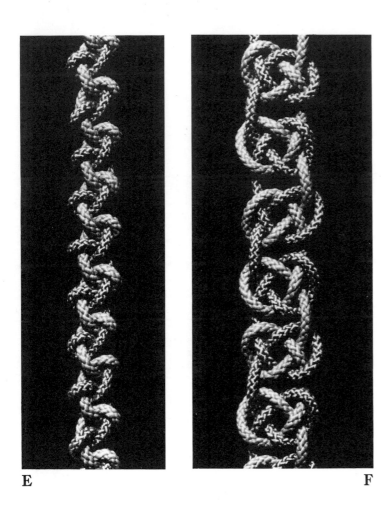

BRAID E

MATERIAL. Synthetic coloured rope from a marine supply store.

NUMBER OF CORDS. Two (one in each of two contrasting colours).

TO MAKE

Work a chain of alternate half hitches.

BRAID F

MATERIAL. Synthetic coloured rope from a marine supply store.

NUMBER OF CORDS. Two (one in each of two contrasting colours).

TO MAKE

The braid is worked in Josephine knots, an attractive fancy knot. Tie the first knot from the left as follows: make a loop with cord 1, as shown in Fa. Now bring cord 2 across the loop, up behind the end of cord 1, over the top part of 1, under the top strand of the loop, under cord 2 where it lies across the loop, and under the lower strand of the loop (Fb). Pull both ends gently and the knot will form itself into a pleasing symmetrical shape. Tie a second knot immediately below the first, but this time tie it from the right: i.e. form a loop with cord 2, then bring cord 1 across it and weave it in and out as before. Continue to tie Josephine knots alternately from left and right to the length required.

E

F

Fa

Fb

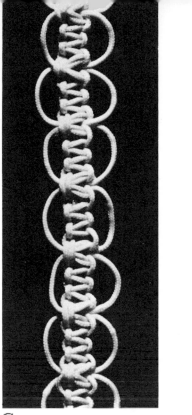

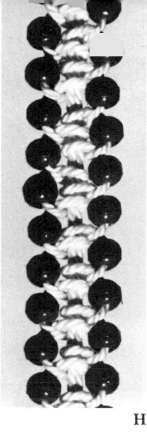

G   H

BRAID G
MATERIALS. Fine nylon cord; coloured plastic twine.
NUMBER OF CORDS. Six (four nylon cords arranged in pairs on either side of two plastic twine cords).
TO MAKE
*Tie a flat knot, using double strands of knotting cords (the nylon cords) and the plastic twine as knotbearing cords. Now leave the outer cords unworked and tie two flat knots, using single strands of nylon as knotting cords, and the plastic twine as knotbearing cords.** Repeat from * to ** to the length required; let the outer nylon cords form regular picot loops at each side.

BRAID H
MATERIALS. Medium silk cord. China beads.
NUMBER OF CORDS. Four.
TO MAKE
Work throughout in half hitches tied alternately with cord 1 over cords 2 and 3, and cord 4 over cords 3 and 2. Before tying each knot, slip a bead on to each knotting cord and slide it up close to the last knot.

BRAID I
MATERIAL. Two-colour sisal string.
NUMBER OF CORDS. Eight.
TO MAKE
Work in an alternate flat knot pattern throughout (i.e. one knot in one row, followed by two knots in the next row, and so on). Space the knots out evenly so a very open-work pattern is created, and let the outside cords form large loops (picots) between the rows of knots.

I

Fringes

FRINGE A

MATERIAL. Cash's cording No. 950.

MEASUREMENTS. Depth of finished fringe, including tassel, 10″.

PREPARATION. Cut cords each 4 ft 4″. Each repeat of the fringe motif requires 12 working ends (i.e. six cut cords), so the total number of cords cut should be a multiple of six.

TO MAKE

Set on cords with ribbed picot headings as follows:
pin cords to working surface in pairs, one cord inside the other so you have a double top loop. Using cords double, slant cords 3 and 4 to the left across cords 1 and 2 then work a diagonal double half hitch with 1 and 2 over 3 and 4. Now slant cords 1 and 2 down to the left across 3 and 4, and work a double half hitch with 3 and 4 over 1 and 2. Lay a holding cord across and work horizontal cording over it with each of the four cords in turn.

Repeat with each pair of cords until all are set on.

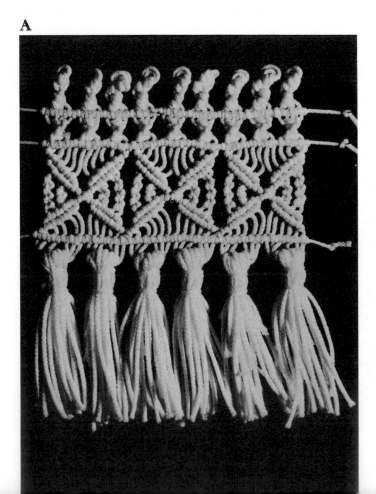

A

Next row: tie four half knots (first half of flat knot) with each group of four cords. Let spiral twist round on itself once.

Next row: introduce a separate leader and work one row of horizontal cording across all cords.

Pattern motif: divide cords into groups of 12. Work on the first group of 12 thus:

*with cord 1 as leader, work a row of diagonal cording slanting down to the right with cords 2, 3, 4, 5 and 6. Work a second row immediately below, with cord 2 as leader. Knot over it cords 3, 4, 5, 6 and 1.

Similarly with cord 12 as leader, work a row of diagonal cording slanting down to the left with cords 11, 10, 9, 8 and 7. Work a second row immediately below, with cord 11 as leader. Knot over it cords 10, 9 8, 7 and 12. Link the centre point of the motif by knotting cord 2 over 11. Work seven alternate half hitches with cords 3 and 4. Work four alternate half hitches with cords 5 and 6. Similarly work seven alternate half hitches with cords 9 and 10, and four alternate half hitches with cords 7 and 8.

Now cord 11 continues as leader; work diagonal cording slanting down to the left over it with cords 1, 6, 5, 4 and 3. With cord 1 as leader, work a second row immediately below, knotting over it cords 6, 5, 4, 3 and 11.

In a similar way work a double row of diagonal cording slanting down to the right with cord 2 as leader for the first row, and knotting over it cords 12, 7, 8, 9 and 10, and cord 12 as leader for second row, knotting over it cords 7, 8, 9, 10 and 2.**

Repeat from * to ** with each group of 12 cords.

Next row: introduce a separate leader and work one row of horizontal cording across all cords.

TO FINISH

Divide cords into groups of six. Work on the first group only:

divide cords into two groups of three and tie in the first half of a flat knot without a central knotbearing core (see page 42, F and G).

Now cut 12 lengths of yarn, each about 10″ (or more for a deeper tassel). Fold cut cords in half, and loop them over the half knot just tied. Complete the tassel as described on page 42, for the Cashmere Shawl.

Repeat with each group of six cords.

Finally trim tassels evenly.

FRINGE B

MATERIAL. Aran knitting wool in two contrasting shades.

MEASUREMENTS. Depth of fringe (excluding fringing) approximately 4¾".

PREPARATION. Cut cords each 5 ft long and set them on to a holding cord in the following colour sequence: one in colour A; two in colour B; two in colour A; two in colour B, and so on, ending with one in colour A. Each repeat of the pattern is worked on eight cord ends (two in colour A, four in colour B, two in colour A).

TO MAKE

Using the cord on the far left as leader, work horizontal cording from left to right across all cords. Reverse the direction of the leader round a pin and work a second row of horizontal cording immediately below, from right to left.

Work on the first group of eight cords:

*with cord 2 as leader, work diagonal cording slanting down to the right with cords 3 and 4. Work a second row immediately below, with cord 1 as leader, and knotting over it cords 3 and 4.

Now work diagonal cording slanting down to the left with cord 7 as leader; knot cords 6 and 5 over it. Work a second row of diagonal cording immediately below with cord 8 as leader, and knotting cords 6 and 5 over it. Now cord 7 continues across the work as a leader at the same slant as before; cording is worked over it with cords 2, 1, 4 and 3 in turn.

Similarly cord 8 continues across the work as a leader, and cording is worked over it with cords 2, 1, 4 and 3. Now cord 2 continues as a leader slanting to the right, and cording is worked over it with cords 5 and 6. Cord 1 continues as leader for a second row below and cords 5 and 6 are knotted over it.**

Repeat from * to ** with each group of eight cords.

Motifs are now linked by using cord 7 from the right-hand motif as a leader slanting down to the left, and cords 2 and 1 of the left-hand motif are knotted over it. Similarly, cord 8 of the right-hand motif becomes leader for the row of diagonal cording immediately below, and cords 2 and 1 of the left-hand motif are knotted over it. Continue to link the motifs together in this way.

Work both odd cords at ends of the fringe as follows:

B

cords at the far left (first motif): use cord 8 as leader, and knot cord 7 over it. Reverse the direction of 8 round a pin and let it continue as the leader, slanting down to the right. Work diagonal cording over it with cord 7.

Cords at the far right (last motif): in a similar way, knot cord 2 over cord 1. Reverse the direction of cord 1 to slant down to the left, and knot cord 2 over it again.***

Several cords by this time will have travelled across the work as leaders; as numbering is becoming confusing divide cords across the row into groups of eight, and re-number them for ease of identification.

Repeat from * to *** twice more (or to the depth of fringe required). At the end of the last repeat, only work the first cording knot on odd cords at either end; i.e. for left-hand cords, knot 7 over 8 once only (do not reverse direction of 8); for right-hand cords, knot 2 over 1 once only.

TO FINISH

With the cord on the far left as leader, work horizontal cording from left to right across all cords. Reverse the direction of the leader round a pin, and work a second row of horizontal cording immediately below, this time from right to left.

Trim fringe evenly.

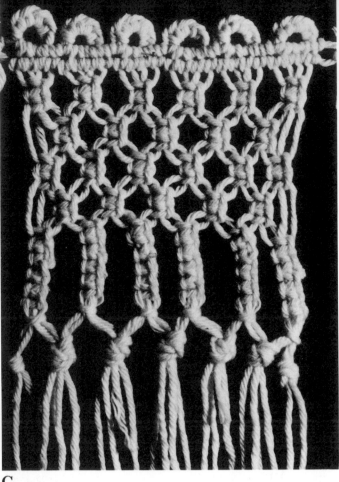

C

Fringes

FRINGE C

MATERIAL. Rug wool.

MEASUREMENTS. Depth of fringe approximately 8″, excluding fringing.

PREPARATION. Cut cords each 70″ long. Set on (in multiples of four working ends) to holding cord by the half hitch scalloped edge method (see page 19).

TO MAKE

Introduce a separate leader and work one row of horizontal cording from left to right across all cords.

*Work two flat knots with each group of four cords to the end of the row.

Next row: leave the first two cords unworked; work two flat knots with each group of four cords to the two last cords; leave these unworked.**

Repeat from * to **.

Next row: work chains of five flat knots with each group of four cords to the end of the row.

TO FINISH

Combine two right-hand cords from each flat knot chain with two left-hand cords of the chain next to it. Tie them together in an overhand knot. Tie the odd pairs of cords at the far left and far right in an overhand knot. Trim fringe evenly.

FRINGE D

MATERIAL. Dishcloth cotton in two contrasting shades.

MEASUREMENTS. Depth of fringe to the tip of the design (excluding fringing) approximately 5½″.

PREPARATION. Cut cords each 1½ yd long and set them in pairs on to a holding cord with overhand picot edging (see page 18) in the following colour sequence: one pair in colour A (two cut cords, giving four working ends); three pairs in colour B; two pairs in colour A; three pairs in colour B; two pairs in colour A, and so on to the end, finishing with one pair of cords in colour A. Each repeat of the pattern is worked on 20 cord ends (four in colour A, twelve in colour B, four in colour A).

TO MAKE

With a separate leader, work one row of horizontal cording across all cords. Begin pattern.

Divide cords into pairs across the work. With cord 2 as a leader slanting down to the left, work a diagonal double half hitch with cord 1 over it. With cord 3 as leader slanting down to the right, work a diagonal double half hitch with cord 4 over it. Continue in this way across cords, knotting each pair of cords with a single diagonal double half hitch, and alternating the direction of each pair. Renumber the cords in groups from 1–4 in the order in which they now lie.

With cord 1 as leader, work a row of horizontal cording with cords 2, 3 and 4. Reverse the direction of cord 1 and work a row of horizontal cording from right to left with the same cords.

With cord 1 as leader slanting down to the right, work a diagonal double half hitch over it with cord 2.

With cord 4 as leader slanting down to the left, work diagonal cording over it with cords 3, 1 and 2.

Now work the centre group of colour B cords: divide cords into three groups of four cords each. Working on the first group, the cords at present lie in the order: 2, 1, 4 and 3.

Let cord 4 continue as leader slanting down to the left, and work diagonal cording over it with cords 1 and 2. Let cord 1 continue as leader slanting down to the right and work a diagonal double half hitch over it with cord 3. Reverse the direction of cord 4 to slant down to the right and work a diagonal double half hitch over it with cord 2. Similarly reverse the direction of cord 1 to slant down to the left and work diagonal cording over it with cords 3, 1 and 2. Letting cord 1 continue as leader slanting down to the right, work a diagonal double half hitch over it with cord 3.

Work similar cording diamond motifs with each of the next two groups of four cords (three motifs in the band). Then work a 2nd band of cording diamonds in a similar way by linking the right-hand cords from motif 1 with the left-hand cords from motif 2, then linking right-hand cords from the 2nd motif with the left-hand cords of the 3rd motif (two motifs in band). Work a 3rd band with only a single motif in it, combining the right-hand cords and left-hand cords of the two motifs in the previous band. You should now have a triangular panel of cording diamonds in colour B, with six cords coming from each side of the triangle.

Work on the left-hand six cords first, linking them to the colour A cords on their left as follows:

with the first of the colour B cords as leader slanting down to the left, work a diagonal double half hitch over it with the first colour A cord on its left. Similarly with the 2nd of colour B cords as leader slanting to the left, work a diagonal double half hitch over it with the first colour A cord.

The 2nd of colour A cords now becomes a leader slanting down to the right, and diagonal cording is worked over it with each of the two colour B cords, the row worked tight against the previous one. The 3rd cord in colour A then becomes leader slanting down to the right, and diagonal cording is worked over it with the two colour B cords. Finally, each of the two colour B cords is used in turn as leader slanting down to the left, and a diagonal double half hitch is worked over each with the fourth colour A cord.

To complete the two-colour cording diamond, the cord on the far right (in colour A) is slanted down to the left following the line of the rest of the motif so far worked, then diagonal cording is worked over it with each of the other colour A cords in turn.

Work two more two-colour cording motifs in a similar way with the other cords in colour B coming from the left-hand side of the triangle.

Now go on to the 2nd group of colour A cords. With the cord on the far left as leader, work a row of horizontal cording across all colour A cords in the group. Reverse its direction and work a 2nd row of horizontal cording.

Divide the cords into two groups of four, and, with the first group, work a band of two-colour cording diamonds to match the first, but this time combine colour A cords with colour B cords from the right-hand side of the triangle, and slant the band down to the left.

Now work the next group of colour B cords in a triangle of cording diamonds, as in the first, and combine its

left-hand cords with the remaining colour A cords on the left to form a band of two-colour cording diamonds slanting down to the right.

Continue in this way across the row.

Finally fill in the space between the bands of two-colour cording diamonds by working a complete large diamond of colour B small cording diamonds. The first row in each large diamond will have just one small diamond, then as cords from either side of the work are brought into the pattern, the 2nd row will have two motifs, and the 3rd will have three motifs.

Decrease the motifs as before, so the next row will have just two motifs, and the final row only one motif.

Work half diamonds with the odd cords at either end of the fringe.

TO FINISH

With a separate leader, work a row of cording on all cords, closely following the shaped outline of the design. Trim the ends to give a fringe of the required depth.

D

Sampler sweater
Shown on front cover

MATERIALS. 938 yards Cash's cording No. 950, from J. & J. Cash Ltd., Coventry.

MEASUREMENTS. To fit average bust size 34/36″; underarm sleeve length 20″, depth of sleeve 7″; centre back length (excluding fringe) approximately 20″.

TENSION CHECK. Over the diamond yoke pattern: approximate depth of diamond 1½″. On main pattern section: a chain of six flat knots measures 2″.

PREPARATION. The back and front of the sweater are made alike. For each piece therefore cut 168 cords (total of 336 cords for the entire sweater) in the following lengths: 112 at 5 ft, 56 at 5 yd. For each side of the sweater cut a holding cord approximately 70″ long (this will form the shoulder and neckline edge). Set cords on in the following order: 40 at 5 ft; (one at 5 yd, three at 5 ft) four times; (three at 5 yd, one at 5 ft) four times; 24 at 5 yd; (one at 5 ft, three at 5 yd) four times; (three at 5 ft, one at 5 yd) four times; 40 at 5 ft. You now have 336 working ends for each side of the sweater.

TO MAKE THE SWEATER FRONT

Work the diamond yoke pattern first.

Divide the cords into groups of eight and work thus:

*with cord 1 as leader slanting down to the right, work diagonal cording over it with cords 2, 3 and 4; with cord 8 as leader slanting down to the left, work diagonal cording over it with cords 7, 6 and 5. Link the two leaders by knotting cord 8 over cord 1.**

Repeat from * to ** with each group of eight cords to the end of the row.

***Return to the first group of eight cords. Cord 8 continues as leader slanting to the left; work cording over it with cords 4, 3 and 2. Cord 1 continues as a leader slanting down to the right; work cording over it with cords 5, 6 and 7.

Repeat this sequence with every group of cords to the end of the row.

Return to the first group of cords.

Reverse the direction of cord 8 round a pin, and with it as leader slanting down to the right, work cording over it with cords 2, 3 and 4.

Link cord 1 of the first motif to cord 8 of the second motif by knotting cord 8 over cord 1.

Cord 8 (of second motif) now continues as leader slanting down to the left and cords 7, 6 and 5 of the first motif are knotted over it.

Repeat this sequence to the end of the row.

The four odd cords at the far right will be worked thus: cord 1 of this motif will continue as leader for diagonal cording slanting to the right, and cords 5, 6 and 7 are worked over it. It is then reversed round a pin and it continues as leader slanting down to the left. Cords 7, 6 and 5 are then knotted over it.

Continue to work thus in the diamond pattern until four complete diamonds have been worked from ***, or until the depth of sleeve is 7″. (If your tension is a little tight, it may be necessary to work another half diamond to reach the required depth.)

Main pattern section. Work on the centre 112 cords only. With the cord on the far left as leader, work a row of horizontal cording from left to right. Reverse the direction of the leader at the end of the row and work a 2nd row of horizontal cording immediately below, this time from right to left.

1st pattern panel: work chains of six flat knots with each group of four cords across the row.

Divider row: with the cord on the far left as leader, work one row of horizontal cording from left to right.

2nd pattern panel: divide cords into groups of 16. Work on the first group thus:

with cord 8 as leader slanting down to the left, work diagonal cording with cords 7, 6, 5, 4, 3, 2 and 1. With cord 7 as leader work a second row of diagonal cording immediately below with cords 6, 5, 4, 3, 2, 1 and 8.

In a similar way work a double row of diagonal cording

Sampler sweater

slanting down to the right with cords 9–16 (cord 9 will be leader for the first row, cord 10 leader for the 2nd row).

Now fill in the centre of the diamond area:

using cords double, tie a half hitch from the left with cords 4 and 5 over 6 and 11; then tie a half hitch from the right with cords 12 and 13 over 6 and 11. Tie a half hitch from the left with cords 8 and 1 over cords 2 and 3; tie a half hitch from the right with cords 4 and 5 over 2 and 3.

Tie a half hitch from the left with cords 12 and 13 over cords 14 and 15; tie a half hitch from the right with cords 16 and 9 over 14 and 15.

Complete this centre pattern by tying a half hitch from the left with cords 4 and 5 over 6 and 11; tie a half hitch from the right with cords 12 and 13 over 6 and 11.

Complete the lower half of the diamond:

reverse the direction of cord 7 round a pin and, with it as leader slanting down to the right, work diagonal cording over it with cords 8, 1, 2, 3, 4, 5 and 6. With cord 8 as leader, work a second row of diagonal cording immediately below, knotting over it cords 1, 2, 3, 4, 5, 6 and 7. Similarly work the other side of the diamond with a double row of cording slanting down to the left: cord 10 will be leader for the first row; cord 9 leader for the second.

Repeat this pattern sequence with each group of 16 cords to the end of the row.

Divider row: with the cord on the far right as leader, work a row of horizontal cording from right to left.

3rd pattern panel: work in alternate flat knot pattern for five rows, being careful not to tie the knots too tightly, but spacing them out regularly to form an attractive lacy pattern.

Divider row: with the cord on the far left as leader, work a row of horizontal cording from left to right.

4th pattern panel: divide cords into groups of 16. Work on the first group thus:

*with cord 8 as leader slanting down to the left, work a row of diagonal cording with cords 7, 6, 5, 4, 3, 2 and 1.

With cord 9 as leader slanting down to the right, work a row of diagonal cording with cords 10, 11, 12, 13, 14, 15 and 16.**

Repeat from * to ** across the row but link V motifs together each time by knotting cord 8 of the motif on the right over cord 9 of the motif on its left.

Return to the first 16 cords. With cord 7 as leader slanting down to the right, work a row of diagonal cording immediately below the previous one with cords 10, 11, 12, 13, 14, 15, 16 and cord 8 of the second motif. With cord 10 as leader slanting down to the left, work diagonal cording immediately below the previous one with cords 6, 5, 4, 3, 2, 1 and 8.

Continue in this way across the row, but again link V motifs together each time by knotting the leader cords from right-hand motifs over the leader cords of left-hand motifs.

Continue until six rows of cording have been worked altogether in each V—you should now have a continuous six-band zigzag of cording going right across the work.

With the half motifs at either end of the row, the leader cords in every row drop down to become knotting cords in subsequent rows.

Divider row: with the cord on the far right as leader, work a row of horizontal cording from right to left.

TO MAKE THE SWEATER BACK
Work exactly as for Sweater Front.

TO FINISH
Trim the holding cords to within an inch of the work, turn to the wrong side and stitch neatly to the back of the set-on cords. Place the back to the front, wrong sides together. Oversew together along the top of the sleeves for 20" in from each cuff edge, thus leaving 20" free in the centre for the neck edge. Stitch underarm seam by oversewing the tips of the diamond cording motifs together along their lower edge.

Oversew the side seams together.

Finally trim the lower fringe to 8" (or depth required). Trim underarm fringe to 6".

Pebble necklace

Designed by Kaffe Fassett

MATERIALS. 1 ball each of parcel string and sisal string; a metal choker ring; 5 medium-sized and 1 large beach pebble with holes in them.

MEASUREMENTS. To fit an average sized neck; depth of necklace—as wished.

TENSION CHECK. Again, variable, depending on the type of string used and the number of strands; as this is a 'free' design it is not vital to have a constant tension measurement.

PREPARATION. Cut 32 lengths of string, each 5 ft for a necklace about 6″ deep (longer if you want it deeper). Set these cords directly on to the choker ring, having the knot of setting-on at the back of the ring (so the knots will not show on the right side of the necklace). Cords can be set on in any arrangement you wish; you may only want a few sisal cords, for instance, or you may wish an equal number of each sort of string.

TO MAKE

With the cord on the far left as leader, work a row of horizontal cording. Divide cords into six unequal groups; it does not matter which have a lot of cords, and which have only a few. Between each group of cords, leave two single cords.

Now tie each multiple group in a flat knot chain for approximately 1″—in every case use single knotting cords, multiple knotbearing central cords. Slide a medium-sized pebble on to each pair of cords between the chains.

With the cord on the far left as leader, work a row of horizontal cording across all cords.

Work chains of two flat knots with each group of four cords to the end of the row.

Divide cords into eight unequal groups.

Work on two centre groups first: work a chain of flat knots with each group (again with single knotting cords) for about 1½″.

Combine a few right-hand cords from the chain on the left with a few left-hand cords from the chain on the right and thread these through the remaining pebble.

Work a chain of flat knots with the remaining cords on the left round the outside of the pebble. Similarly work a chain of flat knots with the remaining cords on the right. Combine both chains under the pebble and work a flat knot chain for about an inch. Tie an overhand knot. Work another inch of flat knots, and tie a second overhand knot.

Work chains of flat knots with the remaining groups of cords to depth required. In a similar way tie an overhand knot about an inch before the end of each chain. Then tie a final overhand knot to complete each chain.

TO FINISH

Trim cords to depth required.

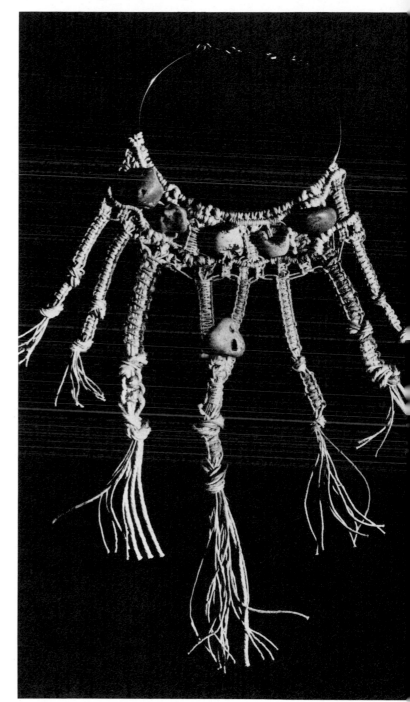

Cashmere shawl

MATERIALS. 1¾ yd cashmere fabric, 48″ wide, from George Harrison and Co (Edinburgh) Ltd, at Harrods; sixteen ½ oz balls Lister's Cashmere yarn.

MEASUREMENTS. Finished shawl measures 42″ square (excluding fringe); depth of fringe approx. 7″, including tassels.

TENSION CHECK. Six horizontal double half hitches worked with double strands measure 1″.

Note. *Yarn is set on double, and used double throughout to give the knotting slightly more 'body' than would otherwise be obtained from single thickness cashmere yarn.*

This shawl is based on Vogue Pattern 8038.

PREPARATION. Cut 492 double lengths of yarn, each 36″ long (i.e. you will in fact cut 984 lengths altogether before arranging them in pairs). Cut a 43″ square from cashmere fabric.

TO MAKE

Turn in a ½″ hem round all raw edges on the fabric square and stitch neatly.

Set on 119 double threads along each edge of the fabric, spacing the threads equally (there will be very approximately ¼″ between each set-on thread). The easiest way to set on the yarn is to thread each pair of threads on to a large-eyed darning needle and stitch them on to the fabric edge (see A).

Pull ends down through the loop, so the finished effect is similar to the normal setting on (see B).

Foundation round: starting around the midpoint of one edge, introduce a separate leader, approx. 180″ long, and work horizontal cording round on all cords. As each corner is reached, set two new double threads on to the

leader. At the end of the round you will have 968 working ends.

Trim the end of the leader cord to about an inch from the last knot, lay the end over the beginning of the round of cording, and oversew firmly to hold together.

Next round: work on each pair of cords thus: using the left-hand cord as leader, work one diagonal double half hitch slanting down to the right with the right-hand cord.

Next round: again beginning around the midpoint of one edge, introduce a separate leader, approx. 184″ long, and work horizontal cording with every cord, as for the foundation round. At each corner, set on another two new cords to the leader.

At the end of the round you will have 984 working ends. Oversew the end of the leader to the beginning of the cording, as in the foundation round.

Now begin pattern. Divide cords into groups of 12. Work on one set of 12 only:

*1st row:** using cord 1 as leader, work diagonal cording slanting down to the right with cords 2, 3 and 4.

Next row: with cord 2 as leader, work a row of diagonal cording immediately below with cords 3, 4 and 1.

With cord 2 still as leader, and continuing the same slant to the right as in the first row, work a row of diagonal cording with cords 5 and 6 (see C).

Now using cord 1 as leader, work a row of diagonal cording immediately below the previous one with cords 5, 6 and 2 (see D).

Work the other half of the V pattern: using cord 12 as leader, work diagonal cording slanting down to the left

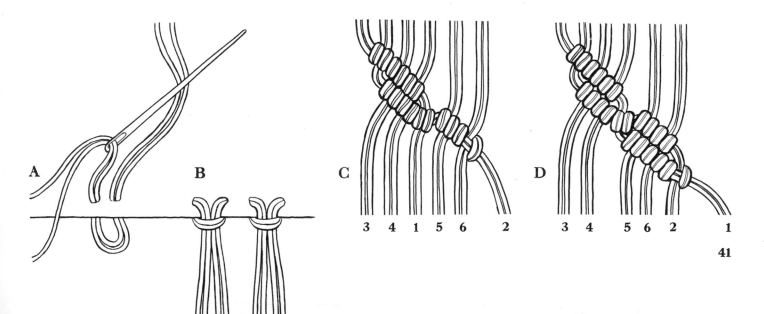

A   B   C   D

3 4 1 5 6   2   3 4   5 6 2   1

Cashmere shawl

with cords 11, 10 and 9. Work a second row immediately below with cord 11 as leader, and knotting cords 10, 9 and 12 over it.

Continue to make the second half of the diagonal cording motif with cord 11 still as leader and knotting over it cords 8 and 7. Work a second row beneath this with cord 12 as leader, and knotting over it cords 8, 7 and 11.

Now link the two double rows of diagonal cording at the tip of the V by working a double half hitch with cord 1 over cord 12 (see E).

Repeat this knotting sequence with each group of 12 cords right round.

Cords for each motif now lie in the following order: 3, 4, 5, 6, 2, 12, 1, 11, 7, 8, 9 and 10.**

2nd pattern round: *** divide cords in groups of 12 again but this time combine cords 1, 11, 7, 8, 9 and 10 from one motif with cords 3, 4, 5, 6, 2 and 12 of the motif on its right.

Loop cords 3 and 4 round cords 9 and 10 to hold the centre of the motif together. Now re-number each group of 12 cords from 1 to 12 as before.

Repeat pattern from * to **. ****
3rd pattern round: repeat from *** to ****
TO FINISH

Make a tassel between each motif on the final round: for each tassel cut 12 lengths of yarn, approx. 9″ long.

Between every motif along the last round worked take the cords on the left and the cords on the right and tie them together in the first half of a flat knot without any central core (see F).

Fold the tassel cords in half and loop them over the half knot just tied. Use any one of the tassel cords to bind tightly round all the cords just below the loop. Secure the end by tying a collecting knot: form a loop at the front of the tassel with the binding cord, then take the cord across the front of the tassel from right to left, round the back and through to the front through the loop. Draw tight (see G).

Make a second tight binding round the tassel about half an inch below the first, finishing with a collecting knot. Make tassels right round in this way. Finally trim the tassels evenly.

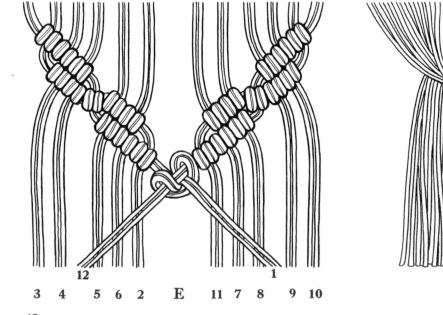

3   4   5   6   2   E   11   7   8   9   10

12 ... 1

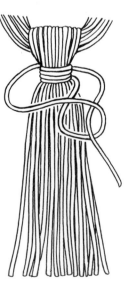

F   G

Braid braces

MATERIALS. 3 balls of heavyweight parcel string; 1 press stud.

DRESS. Vogue Pattern No. 2648, sizes 10–16, in Heather Mills Trelya pure wool crêpe, from Harrods.

MEASUREMENTS. Length of waistband 28″; length of each shoulder braid 36″.

TENSION CHECK. Three flat knots measure 1″.

Braid braces

PREPARATION. For waistband: cut 10 cords, each 6 yd long. Take one of these cords, double it and pin it to the working surface so it forms an inverted V from its midway point. On the right-hand arm of the V, working from centre point down, set on four cords, setting each on with double half hitches (cording) instead of the usual method. On the left-hand arm of the V set on the remaining five cords, also by double half hitches. The holding cords now drop down to become knotting cords, so you have a total of 20 working cords. Number them from 1 to 20 in the order they now lie. **For each shoulder braid:** cut six cords, each 8 yd long. Place four cords together, double them and pin them to the working surface by the top loop. Now cross the left-hand cords over the right-hand cords, making the cross about 2″ down from the top loop. Set on the remaining two cords over this crossed point. This forms a loop by which the braid can be slid on to the waistband.

TO MAKE WAISTBAND

With cord 11 as leader slanting down to the right, work a row of diagonal cording immediately below the set-on edge with cords 12, 13, 14, 15, 16, 17, 18 and 19.

With cord 12 as leader slanting down to the left, work diagonal cording immediately below the other set-on edge with cords 10, 9, 8, 7, 6, 5, 4, 3 and 2.

Now tie a multi-end flat knot, with cords 2, 3, 4, 5 and 6, and cords 15, 16, 17, 18 and 19 as knotting cords, and cords 7, 8, 9, 10, 13 and 14 as the knotbearing central cords.

With cord 12 as leader slanting down to the right, work diagonal cording with cords 2, 3, 4, 5, 6, 7, 8 and 9.

Work a 2nd row of diagonal cording immediately below

with cord 1 as leader slanting down to the right, knotting over it cords 2, 3, 4, 5, 6, 7, 8 and 9.

In a similar way work two rows of cording at the other side of the diamond, with cord 11 as the first leader slanting down to the left, and cord 20 as the second leader, knotting over them cords 19, 18, 17, 16, 15, 14, 13 and 10. Link the tip of the diamond by knotting cords 11 and 20 over cord 12, and then over cord 1.

Work a chain of 12 alternate half hitches with cords 2 and 3.

Tie a chain of two flat knots with cords 4, 5, 6 and 7. On the other side of the diamond, tie two flat knots with cords 14, 15, 16 and 17.

Work a chain of 12 alternate half hitches with cords 18 and 19.

Now repeat the diamond motif, using the same two leaders. Continue in this way working diamond motifs outlined with double rows of cording, and with alternate half hitch chains and flat knots between the diamond motifs, until work measures 28″ (or length required). End after a complete diamond motif has been worked.

Trim ends to about 1″, turn to the wrong side and weave the ends through the back of the knotting. Secure the ends with a spot of fabric glue, if wished.

Sew the press stud to fasten the belt at the centre front.

TO MAKE EACH SHOULDER BRAID

Work two braids alike.

1st pattern section: on first four cords work a spiral of half knots for approximately 6″; on the centre four cords work a chain of flat knots to the same depth; work a spiral of half knots on the last group of four cords.

2nd pattern section: tie single flat knots with each

of the three groups of four cords, in the usual way.

Next row: leave the first two cords unworked; tie flat knots with each of the next two groups of four cords; leave the final two cords unworked.

Next row: tie flat knots with each group of four cords. On the first and last groups of cords, cross cord 1 over cord 2, and cross cord 4 over cord 3. Tie a flat knot (about an inch below the previous flat knot). Repeat the crossing of cords and flat knot sequence twice more.

On the centre four cords tie flat knots, spacing them out at $\frac{1}{2}$" intervals so the last flat knot lines up with the last flat knot tied in the other two groups of cords.

Next row: leave the first two cords unworked; tie a triple knot ($1\frac{1}{2}$ flat knots) with each of the next two groups of four cords; leave the final two cords unworked.

3rd pattern section: tie chains of flat knots spaced out at $\frac{1}{2}$" intervals with the first and last groups of four cords, to $3\frac{1}{2}$".

With the centre group, tie a chain of continuous flat knots (i.e. not spaced out) to the same depth.

4th pattern section: work in alternate flat knot pattern for about $5\frac{1}{2}$".

5th pattern section: work chains of continuous flat knots with the first and last groups of four cords, to about $4\frac{1}{2}$". Tie a chain of flat knots, spaced out at $\frac{1}{2}$" intervals, with the centre four cords.

Work two rows in the alternate flat knot pattern.

6th pattern section: tie chains of flat knots spaced out at $\frac{1}{2}$" intervals with the first and last groups of four cords. On the centre group, cross cord 1 over cord 2, and cross cord 4 over cord 3. Tie a flat knot. Repeat crossing of cords and flat knot sequence until the chain is the same length as the other two in the section.

Work two rows in the alternate flat knot pattern with all cords.

7th pattern section: as first pattern section.

Trim cord ends to about 8".

TO FINISH

Lay waistband flat and decide at what point the braids should be attached at the centre. Lay the braids in position. Take the cord ends of one braid down across the front of the waistband, and up behind it; divide them into two equal groups, cross them at the back and bring them to the front; cross them over again, and finally take them to the back and knot together in a multi-end flat knot. Repeat with the cord ends of the other braid. Do not tie too tightly: the braids should be able to slide fairly easily along the waistband.

Keeping the braids in position, measure up about 11" on one braid from the top edge of the waistband. Cut two cords each 32" long, and set these on at right angles to the braid at this point, directly on to a loop at the edge nearest the centre front (i.e. a loop on the far right of the left-hand braid, or a loop on the far left of the right-hand braid).

Work a chain of flat knots spaced out at $\frac{1}{2}$" intervals with these four working cords for about 4".

Attach the cords to the other braid at a corresponding point, by taking the two centre cords through a loop along the edge of the braid from front to back, then tying the four cords firmly in a flat knot on the wrong side of the work. Trim the ends neatly.

Finally cut four cords, each 8" long. Double each length and set them on to the loops along the lower edge of the horizontal crosspiece just worked. Tie each pair of cords in an overhand knot, and fray out the ends, if wished.

Apron

MATERIALS. 2 balls of jute string (or any other type of fairly soft, fine string); 3 yd ribbon braid, 1″ wide.

DRESS. Miss Vogue Pattern 8132, sizes 6–14, in Liberty Tana lawn.

MEASUREMENTS. Length of apron (excluding fringe) 16″; width of yoke 6″; width of skirt section 9½″.

TENSION CHECK. Chain of five flat knots, tied with double thickness cords, is 1″.

PREPARATION. Cut 52 cords, each 4 yd long; cut 24 cords each 3 yd long. Set the 52 cords on to a holding cord of about 1 ft.

Note. *Unless otherwise stated, cords are to be used double throughout.*

TO MAKE

Introduce a separate leader and work a row of horizontal cording across all cords.

Divide cords into groups of four double cords.

*Work on the first group of double cords:
tie a chain of four flat knots.

Work on the second group of double cords:
with cord 4 as leader slanting down to the left, work a row of diagonal cording with cords 3, 2 and 1. With cord 3 as leader, work a second row of diagonal cording immediately below with cords 2, 1 and 4.

Work on the third group of four double cords:
tie a chain of four flat knots.

Work on the fourth group of four double cords:
with cord 1 as leader slanting down to the right, work a row of diagonal cording with cords 2, 3 and 4. With cord 2 as leader, work a second row of diagonal cording immediately below with cords 3, 4 and 1.**

From * to ** is the pattern. Repeat it twice using other groups of cords across the row.

Complete the row by tying a chain of four flat knots with the last group of four double cords.

Divider row: with the cord on the far right as leader, work a row of horizontal cording across all cords.

Divide the cords into groups of four double cords again.

Work on the first group of four double cords:
tie a chain of 11 flat knots.

Now work across the row as follows:

tie chains of two flat knots with each of the next three groups of four double cords; leave the next four double cords unworked. * Repeat from *** to ****; tie chains of two flat knots with each of the next three groups of double cords.

Tie a chain of 11 flat knots with the last group of double cords.

Beneath the two-knot chains just worked, continue as follows:

leave the first two cords unworked, tie chains of two flat knots with each of the next two groups of four double cords; leave the next eight double cords unworked; tie chains of two flat knots with each of the next two groups of four double cords; leave the next eight double cords unworked; tie chains of two flat knots with each of the next two groups of four double cords; leave the last two cords unworked.

Now with the first four double cords tie a chain of four flat knots; tie a chain of two flat knots with next four double cords; leave the next 12 cords unworked; tie a chain of two flat knots with the next four double cords; leave the next 12 cords unworked; tie a chain of two flat knots with the next four double cords; tie a chain of four flat knots with the last four double cords.

Now return to the first area of unworked cords, and work a cording diamond as follows:

number cords from 1 to 14 (cords 1 and 14 will be taken from the last chains of flat knots worked either side of the area; cords 2 through to 13 are the cords left unworked). With cord 7 as leader slanting down to the left, work diagonal cording over it with cords 6, 5, 4, 3, 2 and 1. With cord 8 as leader slanting down to the right, work diagonal cording over it with cords 9, 10, 11, 12, 13 and 14.

With cord 9 as leader slanting down to the left, work a row of diagonal cording over it with cords 6, 5 and 4. With cord 10 as leader slanting down to the left, work a second row of diagonal cording immediately below with cords 6, 5 and 4. With cord 11 as leader work a third row of diagonal cording, also with cords 6, 5 and 4.

With cord 3 as leader slanting down to the right, work

Apron

diagonal cording over it with cords 9, 10 and 11. Work two more rows of diagonal cording immediately below with these same three cords, first over cord 2 as leader, then over cord 1.

Continuing in a similar way at the right-hand side of the diamond, work three rows of diagonal cording slanting down to the right with cords 12, 13 and 14. Cord 6 will be the leader for the first row, cord 5 the leader for the second row, cord 4 the leader for the third row.

Complete the lower part of the diamond by working three rows of diagonal cording slanting to the left with cords 3, 2 and 1. Cord 12 will be leader for the first row, cord 13 the leader for the second row, cord 14 the leader for the third row.

Finally reverse the direction of cord 7 round a pin and work a row of diagonal cording over it slanting down to the right with cords 9, 10, 11, 12, 13 and 14. Reverse the direction of cord 8 round a pin, and work a row of diagonal cording over it slanting down to the left with cords 6, 5, 4, 3, 2 and 1.

Note. *As you will see, the cords from the left of the diamond have crossed to the right, and cords from the right have crossed over to the left.*

Work a second cording diamond with the other group of unworked cords.

Complete the lower part of the pattern panel to match the upper part, in alternating chains of two flat knots.

Divider row: with the cord on the far left as leader, work a row of horizontal cording across all cords. Divide cords into groups of four double cords. Work on each group as follows:

with cord 4 as leader slanting down to the left, work diagonal cording with cords 3, 2 and 1.

Divider row: with the cord on the far right as leader, work a row of horizontal cording across all cords.

*With cord 4 as leader slanting down to the left, work diagonal cording with cords 3, 2 and 1. With cord 5 as leader slanting down to the right, work diagonal cording with cords 6, 7 and 8.

Reverse the direction of cord 4 round a pin and work diagonal cording over it slanting down to the right with cords 1, 2 and 3. Similarly reverse the direction of cord 5 and work diagonal cording over it slanting down to the left with cords 8, 7 and 6.**

Repeat from * to ** twice.

With the next group of four double cords, tie a chain of five flat knots.

Repeat from * to ** three times.

Divider row: with the cord on the far left as leader, work a row of horizontal cording across all cords. Cut a separate leader, approximately 18″ long. Pin this in position across the work. Set on the remaining 24 cords to this leader, 12 on the left of the section just worked, 12 on the right, to give the increased width for the skirt section of the apron.

Now work horizontal cording over this leader, with the central (yoke) cords.

Work on the first 12 cords (left-hand side panel):

*with cord 4 as leader slanting to the left, work diagonal cording with cords 3, 2 and 1. Reverse the direction of cord 4 and work diagonal cording slanting to the right with cords 1, 2 and 3.

With the next four double cords tie a chain of four flat knots. With the next four double cords, use cord 9 as the leader, slanting down to the right, and work diagonal cording with cords 10, 11 and 12. Reverse the direction of cord 9 and work diagonal cording slanting to the left with cords 12, 11 and 10.**

Tie a multi-end flat knot with the next 12 double cords (four double cords each side as knotting cords; four double cords as the central knotbearing core).*

Repeat from *** to ****.

With the next group of four double cords tie 16 half knots. Let the spiral twist round on itself after every fourth knot.

Repeat from *** to **** twice.

Repeat from * to ** with the last 12 double cords.

On the first 12 double cords, use cord 12 as leader and work a row of horizontal cording from right to left to the end of the row.

On the last group of 12 double cords, use cord 1 as leader and work a row of horizontal cording from left to right to the end of the row.

Now with the cord on the far left as leader, work a row of horizontal cording across all cords.

The side panels of the apron are now worked separately as follows:

working on the left-hand side panel, divide cords into three groups of four double cords. With the first group, work six rows of diagonal cording slanting to the right, using the cord on the far left as leader for each row. After the sixth row, reverse the direction of the last leader used and then work six rows of diagonal cording slanting down to the left, this time using the cord on the far right as leader for each row.

Repeat this pattern sequence with each of the other two groups of four double cords, then work a row of horizontal cording across all 12 double cords, using the cord on the far left as leader.

With the first group of four double cords, tie a chain of three flat knots. With the second group of four double cords tie eight half knots. With the third group of four double cords, tie a chain of three flat knots.

Work a row of horizontal cording across all cords with the cord on the far left as leader.

Now repeat the six-band cording braid pattern worked previously.

Work a row of horizontal cording across all cords with the cord on the far left as leader.

With cord 6 as leader slanting down to the left, work diagonal cording with cords 5, 4, 3, 2 and 1. With cord 7 as leader slanting down to the right, work diagonal cording with cords 8, 9, 10, 11 and 12.

Tie two multi-end flat knots with cords 2, 3, 4, 5, 8, 9, 10 and 11 (two double knotting cords from each side, four double central knotbearing core cords).

With cord 6 as leader slanting down to the right, work diagonal cording with cords 1, 2, 3, 4 and 5.

With cord 7 as leader slanting down to the left, work diagonal cording with cords 12, 11, 10, 9 and 8.

With the cord on the far left as leader, work a row of horizontal cording across all cords.

On each group of four double cords, with cord 4 as leader slanting down to the left, work three rows of diagonal cording slanting down to the left, using the cord on the far right as leader for each row.

Tie two flat knots and an overhand knot to finish. Repeat this entire section for the right-hand side panel.

Now work on the central skirt panel as follows:

work a pattern panel as for the last pattern panel of the yoke section, followed by a row of horizontal cording.

Work a pattern panel as for the second last pattern panel of the yoke section, followed by two rows of horizontal cording.

Now work a panel of cording leaf motifs:

on the first group of four double cords, work two rows of diagonal cording slanting down to the right, with the cord on the far left as leader for each row. Work two rows of diagonal cording slanting down to the left with the next four double cords, using the cord on the far right as the leader for each row.

Link these two groups together by knotting the leader from the left-hand group over the leader from the right-hand group. Now work two rows of diagonal cording slanting to the left on the first group, using the cord on the far right as leader for each row. Work two rows of diagonal cording slanting to the right on the second group, with the cord on the far left as leader for each row.

Work two more leaf motifs across the row in a similar way; leave the next group of four double cords unworked for the moment. Work three leaf motifs with each group of eight double cords to the end of the row.

Work a second band of leaf motifs immediately below the band just worked, linking the tips of the motifs together if wished by knotting one leader over another.

Return to the cords left unworked in the centre and work 11 rows of diagonal cording slanting to the left, with the cord on the far right as leader for each row.

Work a row of horizontal cording across all cords.

Work as follows for the next pattern band:

chain of five flat knots; spiral of 12 half knots; two cords unworked; chain of five flat knots; two cords unworked; chain of five flat knots; four cords unworked; spiral of 12 half knots; four cords unworked; chain of five flat knots; two cords unworked; chain of five flat knots; two cords unworked; spiral of 12 half knots; chain of five flat knots.

Work two rows of horizontal cording.

Work a pattern panel as for the last pattern panel of the yoke section, followed by a row of horizontal cording. With each group of four double cords, work a cording braid pattern as worked for the side panels, but only work four rows of diagonal cording each time (instead of six).

Work a row of horizontal cording.

Work crossovers of diagonal cording on each group of eight double cords, with a chain of three flat knots worked on the centre four double cords. Have half motifs at the beginning and end of the row, also at either side of the central flat knot chain.

Finally divide the cords across the row into groups of four double cords. On each group tie a flat knot followed by an overhand knot to finish.

TO FINISH

Trim the fringe to the length required. Cut ribbon braid into three equal lengths. Stitch a length to the top of each side panel to form waist ties. Stitch one end of the third length to the left-hand top corner of the yoke, the other end to the right-hand top corner of the yoke. Trim holding and leader cords, turn to the wrong side and secure with a few neat stitches.

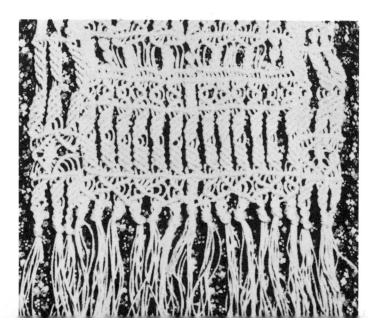

Vest top

MATERIALS. 159 yards Nylofil nylon cord size 2H.
DRESS. Miss Vogue Pattern 8132, in Liberty Tana lawn.
MEASUREMENTS. Vest should fit an average bust size 34/36"; the waistband can be made longer or shorter as required for a neat fitting. Similarly, the braids which go up either side of the bib front, over the shoulder, and down to meet the waistband at the back can be made longer or shorter as required.
TENSION CHECK. Chain of four flat knots is $\frac{3}{4}$".
PREPARATION. For waistband: cut ten lengths of cord at 6 yd each, one at 6 yd 6", and one at 6 yd 1 ft. Pin 6 yd 6" length to a working surface centrally, so it can be used as a holding cord. Set on the other cords, setting on the 6 yd 1 ft length first and work it to form an alternate half hitch scalloped edging (see page 19). This will form a chain loop across the edge to be used as the centre back fastening of the waistband. When all the cords are set on, each end of the holding cord drops down to become a working cord: you should now have 24 working ends.
For bib front: cut 19 lengths at $1\frac{1}{2}$ yd each, and one at 2 yd. Pin the 2 yd length centrally to the working surface so it can be used as a holding cord. Set the other cords on to it with a simple picot edging (see page 18). When all the cords are set on, each end of the holding cord drops down to become a working cord. You should now have 40 working ends.
For each shoulder braid: cut four lengths at 7 yd each. Place all four cords together, and pin to the working surface so you have a quadruple top loop.

TO MAKE THE WAISTBAND

*1st row: work four flat knots with each group of four cords to the end of the row.
2nd row: leave the first two cords unworked; work single flat knots with each group of four cords to the last two cords; leave these two cords unworked.
3rd row: work single flat knots with each group of four cords to the end of the row.
4th row: leave the first two cords unworked; work four flat knots with each group of four cords to the last two cords; leave these two cords unworked.
5th row: work single flat knots with each group of four cords to the end of the row.

6th row: leave the first two cords unworked; work single flat knots with each group of four cords to the last two cords; leave these two cords unworked.**
Repeat from * to ** 9 times (or until the waistband is the length required).
Next row: with the cord on the far left as leader, work a row of horizontal cording across all cords.
Work on first eight cords: divide them into two groups of four and work an alternate half hitch chain, with four-strand knotting cords. When the chain is about 8" long tie an overhand knot to finish, and trim the ends to about an inch from the overhand knot.
In a similar way, tie a double alternate half hitch chain with the next four cords; then tie another double alternate half hitch chain with the following four cords. Finally, tie a quadruple alternate half hitch chain with the last eight cords.

TO MAKE THE BIB FRONT
Work in the pattern of the waistband until five rows of four flat knot chains have been worked.
Next row: with the cord on the far left as leader, work one row of horizontal cording from left to right.
Unpin the work from the board, turn it to the wrong side and work another row of horizontal cording across the lower edge, with the cord on the far left as leader. Trim the ends to about $\frac{1}{2}$" from this last row of cording.

TO MAKE THE SHOULDER BRAIDS (make two alike)
Tie a continuous chain of Josephine knots (see page 30), using four-strand cords; tie the knots alternately from the left and right. When the chain is about 30" long, stop knotting and trim the ends to about 8".

TO FINISH
Stitch the lower edge of the bib front centrally to the top edge of the waistband. Stitch each shoulder braid down each side of the front bib, and to the top edge of the front waistband. Secure the other ends of each braid to the top edge of the back waistband by weaving the cord ends through the waistband to the back of the work, then, working on four cords at a time, tie a two-knot flat knot chain.
Trim the ends to within an inch of the last flat knot, and secure this chain to the wrong side of the waistband with a few overcasting stitches.

Yoked smock

MATERIALS. 118½ yd Cash's striped cording 917, from J. & J. Cash Ltd., Coventry; 1 yd each of as many colours of Cash's striped cording as wished; 15 buttons, each about ½" in diameter.
DRESS. Vogue Pattern No. 7952, sizes 8–16, in Tootal's gingham.
MEASUREMENTS. To fit bust size 34/36". Depth of yoke approximately 10". Depth of cuff 2".
TENSION CHECK. Two flat knots measure ½".
PREPARATION. For the yoke: each side is worked in a similar way over a pattern piece. Take the pattern piece for the yoke, trim away any seam allowance on the pattern, then pin the piece to your working surface. Cut a holding cord of about 18" and pin it in place along the shoulder edge of the pattern piece. Let the left-hand end of the holding cord come down to follow the curve of the neckline edge, and pin it in place. Similarly let the right-hand end of the holding cord come down to follow the armhole curve, and pin it in place. Now cut 10 cords, each 2 yd 1 ft long, and set these on to the holding cord along the shoulder edge. Cut another six cords, each 1½ yd long and set these on to the holding cord along the neck edge, positioning them at the centre front edge. The other side of the yoke will be prepared in a similar way, but the pattern piece must be reversed.
For each cuff (both made alike): cut six cords, each 2 yd long. Cut a holding cord about 6". Set these cords on to the holding cord with simple picot edging (see page 18), so picot loops (for buttons) are about ½" deep.

TO MAKE THE YOKE

Make two pieces alike, but remember to reverse the pattern piece for the second section so you have a left and a right yoke.
Work in a two-knot alternate flat knot pattern throughout (i.e. alternate blocks of two flat knots). At each side edge loop the working cords round the holding cords between each row of knots. As the work becomes level with the set-on cords at the centre front neck edge, bring them into the pattern.
Tie the knots fairly tightly and close together near the top of the yoke. Gradually increase the distance between knots and rows as you work down to achieve shaping. Keep the centre front edge straight all the time.
Right-hand yoke section only: let the knotting cord nearest to the centre front edge form picot loops at nine evenly-spaced intervals (approx. ¾") along the edge, for button loops.
Finish the yoke by working a row of horizontal cording across all cords, using the cord on the far left as leader, and following the outline of the pattern piece closely.

TO MAKE THE CUFFS (make two alike)

Work in pattern as for the yoke until the cuff is 7" long. Work a row of horizontal cording to the end, with the cord on the far left as leader.

TO FINISH

Trim the ends of the yoke and cuff pieces to about 1", turn to the wrong side of the work and secure with a line of machine stitching or running stitches. Make up the dress according to instructions, using a plain lining fabric for the yoke sections (remember to add seam allowances to the pattern piece if these have been trimmed away). Omit cuffs. Place the macramé yoke sections in position on the right side of the fabric yoke. Oversew together round the armhole, shoulder, neck and centre front edges. Sew buttons to the left front centre edge opposite the button loops. Sew each macramé cuff in position to each sleeve end. Sew three buttons to each cuff, opposite the picot button loops (use two loops for fastening each button).
Between every chain of flat knots along the lower edge of the yoke set on a different coloured length of striped cording, to make a long fringe.

Child's sailor top

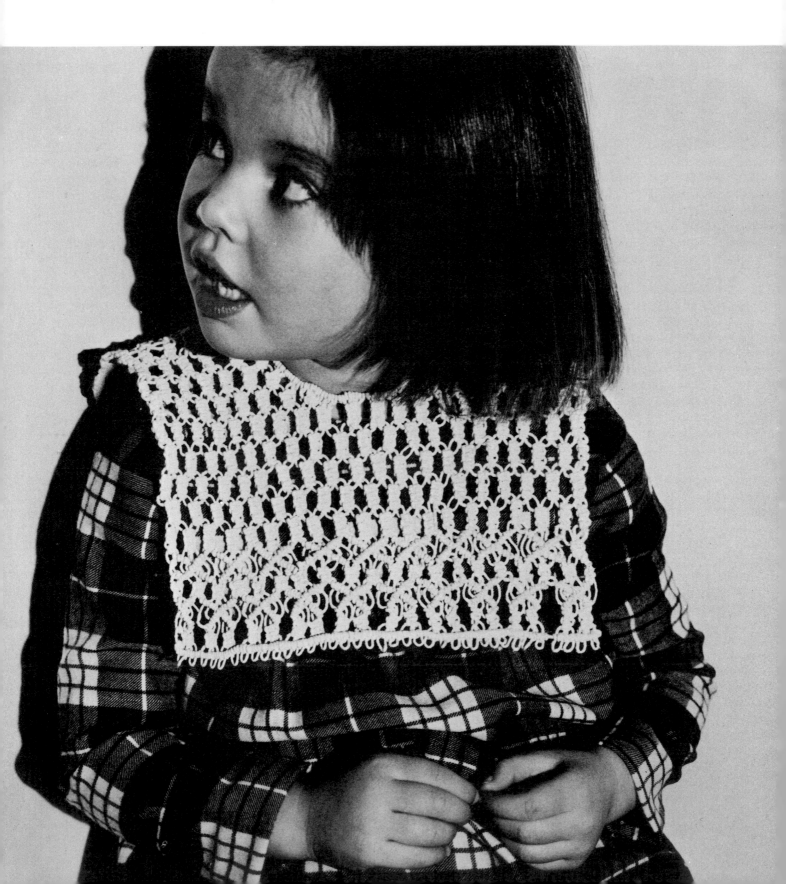

MATERIALS. 1 ball W. H. Smith C3 medium string; three press studs.

DRESS. Vogue Pattern No. 6032, sizes 2–6, in checked Viyella.

MEASUREMENTS. Finished bib measures approximately 8½″ across, 14″ in total depth (from front to back).

TENSION CHECK. Three flat knots measure ½″.

PREPARATION. Cut 24 cords at 3 yd, 14 at 1½ yd. Cut a holding cord approximately 18″, and set cords on to it with simple picot edging (see page 18) in the following order: 12 at 3 yd, 14 at 1½ yd, 12 at 3 yd.

TO MAKE

1st row: Work two flat knots with each group of four cords to the end of the row.

Divide the cords into nine groups of eight (have the odd four cords at the end).

Work on the first group of eight cords:

*work a crossover of diagonal cording with cords 1 and 8 as leaders, knotting 1 over 8 at the crossover point.** Work from * to ** eight more times. Work a half motif with the four cords at the end of the row.

Next row: work two half hitches from the right with cord 2 over cord 1; tie two flat knots with each group of four cords to the last two cords; tie two half hitches from the right with these two last cords.

Next row: work eight-cord crossovers of diagonal cording as before, but this time have the half motif with four cords at the beginning of the row.

Now begin the main pattern.

*Next row: work three flat knots with each group of four cords to the end of the row.

Next row: work three flat knots with the first six cords, having single knotting cords, and a central knotbearing core of four cords; tie three flat knots with each group of four cords to the last six cords; tie three flat knots with these last six cords, having single knotting cords and a centre knotbearing core of four cords.**

Repeat from * to ** once, then work the first row of the pattern again.

Divide for the neck opening. Keeping in pattern, work the first six chains of flat knots, then on the next group of four cords tie only two flat knots; on the next group of four cords tie only one flat knot.

Leave the next 12 cords unworked, then tie one flat knot with the next four cords, two flat knots with the following four cords, then complete the row in the pattern (six chains of flat knots).

Next row: still in pattern, work the first six chains of flat knots, then work two flat knots with the next group of four cords; leave the next 24 cords unworked; work two flat knots with the next four cords, then complete the row in pattern.

Next row: six chains of flat knots; leave the next 28 cords unworked; six chains of flat knots.

Now cut a separate length of string, approximately 14″ long (this will form the neck edge of the bib). Lay this cord on top of the unworked area of cords in the centre, close to the last knots tied, and following the curve of the shaped edge. Work cording over this leader with all the central cords; fill in the gaps on the leader where necessary by working half hitches with the cords nearest to hand.

This completes the front of the bib to the shoulder edge. Now pin the leader cord to form the curve of the back neck. Cut 22 cords each 1½ yd, and set on to the leader, 11 for the left back, 11 for the right back.

Work on the left back first.

Next row: leave the first two cords unworked; work chains of two flat knots with each of the next two groups of four cords, then work four chains of three flat knots (the last chain will use the first four of the new cords). Now continuing round the shaped neck edge, work five chains of two flat knots each: the first of these chains will use two cords from the last three-knot chain worked and the next two new set-on cords.

Keeping in alternate flat knot pattern, work two rows of two flat knot chains round the yoke centre area, but have three knots in the chains nearer the outside edge; this is necessary to achieve the shaping for the shoulder slope. Provided you maintain the continuity of the alternate pattern, it does not matter which chains have two knots, and which have three.

When you are satisfied shaping is complete, and all the cords line up evenly, continue in the pattern until the back measures the same as the front yoke.

Work the right back to match, reversing all shaping.

TO FINISH

Using the cord on the far left as leader, work one row of horizontal cording across all cords.

Trim every second cord close to the last row of cording, turn, and stitch to the wrong side of the work to secure. Loop the remaining cords on to the wrong side of work to simulate the picot edging at the beginning, and stitch to secure. Trim the holding and leader cords to within ½″ of the work, turn to the wrong side and secure with a few stitches.

Sew press studs to the centre back edge to fasten, placing the first press stud at the neck edge, the other two at 2″ intervals below.

Child's pinafore

MATERIALS. 2 balls of W. H. Smith C3 thin string; 2 yd of ribbon, 1″ wide; a medium crochet hook.

DRESS. Vogue Pattern No. 6088, sizes ½–4, in flower-printed Viyella.

MEASUREMENTS. To fit size 4; length of pinafore 16″.

TENSION CHECK. Approximately three rows of flat knots over the lacy pattern measure 1″.

PREPARATION. With the crochet hook and string, work two crochet chains each approximately 50″ long. The back and front of the pinafore are made alike. For each side, therefore, cut cords as follows: cut 16 cords each 3½ yd long, 10 cords each 3 yd long. Take the paper pattern piece for the pinafore section. Trim away any seam allowance on the pattern, then pin the piece to your working surface. Now take one crochet chain and very carefully pin this in position round the outside edge of the pattern; begin pinning at the lower left-hand corner. Take the chain up the left side edge to the shoulder, across the shoulder, down round the neckline, up to the other shoulder and across it, then down the right-hand side edge to the right-hand lower corner. Do not pin the chain along the hem edge. Set eight cords directly on to the crochet chain at the shoulder edges, spacing the cords evenly across the edge. Set the remaining ten cords on to the lower curve of the neckline.

TO MAKE

Work in the alternate flat knot pattern throughout. Between every row the end cords should be looped through the crochet chains at the armhole and neck edges. The two shoulder sections will be knotted first; the neck edge cords should be taken into the pattern when they are reached.

Keep knots fairly tightly tied near the top of the pinafore, and gradually increase the distance between knots and rows to achieve the slightly flared shaping of the pinafore skirt.

TO FINISH

With the cord on the far left as leader, work a row of horizontal cording across all cords, following the line of the hem edge of the paper pattern as closely as possible. Trim the ends to about 2″.

Unpin work from the board, remove the paper pattern, then turn the work on its side and pin to the board so the hem edge is running vertically. Cut a length of string about 3 yd long. Double it and pin the top loop immediately above the lower edge of the pinafore. Now using the left-hand cord as a knotting cord, tie half hitches tightly down the entire hem edge, catching in the loose ends as you work. About 2″ from the end of the hem, turn the remaining ends up so they too are caught into the half hitch chain. When the chain is complete, trim the end of the knotting cord to about 1″, turn to the wrong side and secure it with a few neat overcasting stitches.

Stitch pinafore back to the front at the shoulder edges. Cut the ribbon in half and thread each length through the side edges of the pinafore to use as ties.

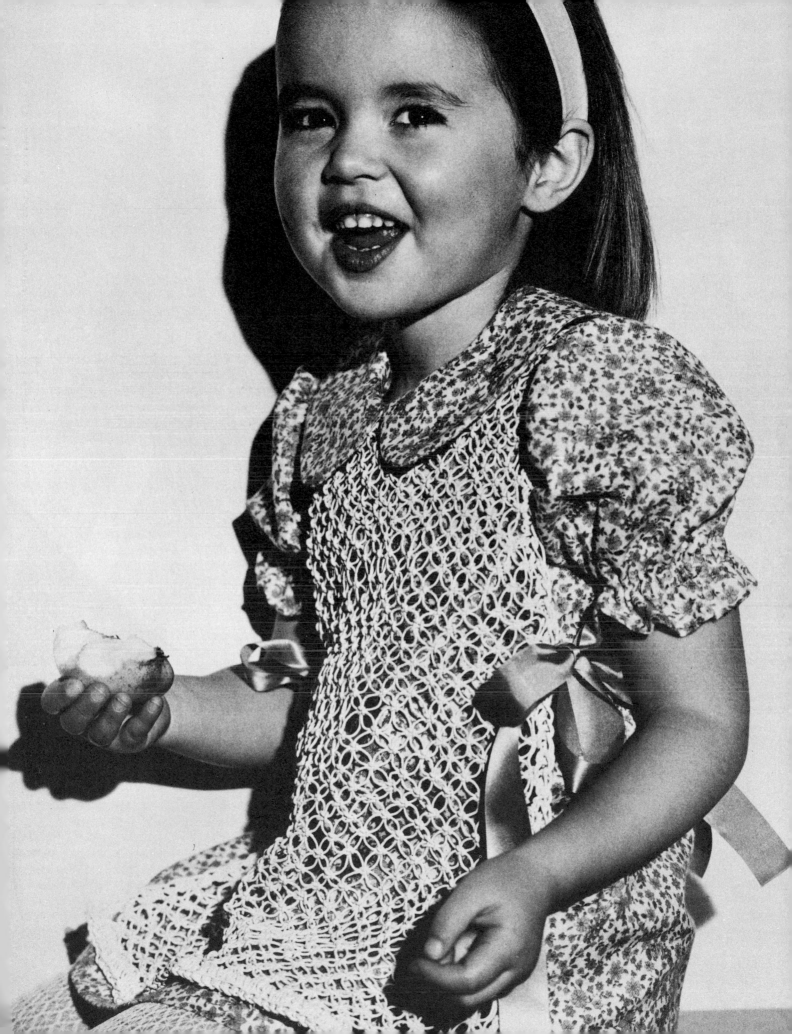

Aran sweater

MATERIALS. 16 oz Mahony's Blarney Bainin wool.

MEASUREMENTS. Sweater will comfortably fit a bust size 34/36″; length of sweater at centre front, approximately 26″.

TENSION CHECK. Over open-work diamond pattern (yoke section) each 'leg' of the diamond measures $\frac{1}{2}$″; each cording diamond motif measures 1″ square.

PREPARATION Cut 86 cords, each 6 yd long. Set these in pairs on to a triple thickness holding cord of about 50″.

Note. *The entire sweater is worked as a flat rectangle, from the neck edge down. The shaping for the neckline, shoulders and yoke section is achieved after the knotting is complete, by drawing up the holding cord.*

Cords are used double throughout; therefore you now have 86 double thickness knotting cords.

TO MAKE

Begin open-work diamond pattern:

working on the *wrong* side, divide the cords into pairs and work a diagonal double half hitch with each left-hand cord over each right-hand cord.

Re-divide the cords into pairs so each right-hand cord of the last row is combined with each left-hand cord. Leaving an area of about $\frac{1}{2}$″ of unworked cords from the last row, work another row of diagonal double half hitches this time knotting each right-hand cord over each left-hand cord.

Continue in this way working an alternate pattern of single diagonal double half hitches until 12 rows have been worked.

Now divide for armholes as follows.

Next row: keeping in pattern, work ten knots. Continue on this set of cords only.

Next row: leave first cord unworked; work nine knots.

Next row: leave first two cords unworked; work eight knots.

Continue in this way, dropping a cord from each side until the row with only a single knot in it is worked.

In a similar way, work four more V patterns, first on the next 12 cords (six knots in the first row), then on the next 22 cords (11 knots in the first row), then on 12 cords, and finally on 20 cords.

The two V shapes worked on 12 cords will form the shoulders and armholes of the sweater. Trim the cord ends from these V shapes and, if necessary, stitch the ends neatly to the last knot to conceal and strengthen.

Now turn the work to the right side.

Plait three strands of yarn together to make a length of about 46″. Lay this across the work so it is just touching the tips of the V shapes; work horizontal cording over it with all the remaining cords (i.e. those not trimmed

away). As you work, between the double half hitches set on 82 new cords each 8 ft long. Set these on in pairs as before. At the end of the row you should have a total of 144 working (double) ends.

Work on groups of eight cords:

with cord 5 as leader slanting down to the left, work diagonal cording over it with cords 4, 3, 2 and 1.

Work three more rows of diagonal cording on these same four cords, one below the other, using cord 6 as leader for the 2nd row, cord 7 as leader for the 3rd row, and cord 8 as leader for the 4th row.

Work across the row in this way.

In the 2nd row, the four left-hand cords of each motif of the previous row are combined with the four right-hand cords of the motif next to it. The same cording diamond as before is then worked. Leave an area of about $\frac{1}{4}$″ of unworked cords between the motifs. Let the unworked cords at either end of the 2nd and other even-numbered rows form even curves at the ends of the rows.

Continue in this way working an alternate pattern of cording diamonds.

When the cording diamond section of the work measures 12″ (or length of sweater required) introduce a separate double thickness leader and work horizontal cording across all cords.

TO FINISH

Trim cords to about $\frac{1}{2}$″, press to the wrong side and secure with a line of running stitches. Trim the leader cords in the centre of the work and at the end to about 1″, press to the wrong side and secure with a few neat overcasting stitches.

Now take hold of both ends of the neck edge holding cord and pull gently, to draw in the work. Try on the sweater (the open edges meet at centre back) and adjust the gathering round the neck edge until it fits neatly and evenly. Tie an overhand knot at either end of the holding cord to stop the gathering coming undone. Take off the sweater, and stitch each overhand knot firmly to the first set-on cords at either end to give further strength to the edge. Adjust gathers evenly. Stitch the centre back seam from the lower edge to the top of the cording diamond section.

Plait the ends of the neck edge holding cord into a three-strand plait; use them as ties for the back neck.

Make 15 pompons, each $2\frac{1}{2}$″ in diameter. Stitch five at intervals round each armhole edge, one at the centre front neck edge, one at each shoulder, one to the centre back neck (on the left back), and the other one halfway down the centre back opening edge (on the left back). Set on a loop of yarn to the edge opposite this last pompon to fasten round it; this closes the opening.

Beaded poncho

MATERIALS. 9 balls W. H. Smith C3 medium string; approximately 500 wooden beads, from Ells and Farrier, 5 Princes Street, London W.1.

MEASUREMENTS. Length of poncho at the centre front 30″; width at widest point, about 30″.

TENSION CHECK. Chain of five flat knots measures 1½″.

PREPARATION. The entire poncho is worked flat in one piece, starting at the shoulder edges and working either side for front and back. You will therefore need an extensive area of suitable working surface, and preferably one which will take pins easily. A large piece of soft wood placed on the floor is probably most convenient; alternatively a well-padded table could be used. Cut 124 cords, each 15 ft 6″ long. Lay two groups of 48 cords singly side by side on your working surface, leaving a gap of 8″ between the two groups. Now measure the midway point of the cords and place a line of pins right across all the cords at this point. This line of pins marks the shoulder line. Tie a row of four-end flat knots across on this line, removing the pins as you work. Space out the knots so the measurement of each shoulder is about 24″. Work now proceeds on either side of this shoulder line of knots.

TO MAKE

In the alternate flat knot pattern, work four more rows of knots on either side of the shoulder line with each group of cords, spacing out the knots in a fairly open pattern. Now cut two holding cords, each about 12″ long, one for the centre front neck edge, the other for the centre back neck edge.

Lay these holding cords in position between the shoulder cords, looping each end of each holding cord round the nearest convenient knot. Set 14 new cords (the remaining 28 cut cords from Preparation) on to each holding cord. Keeping in pattern, work a row of flat knots across all the cords to link the shoulder cords to the new cords. You should now have a total of 124 working ends on the front of the poncho, and 124 ends for the back.

Continue in the alternate flat knot pattern for two more rows for both back and front.

Now work in the main pattern, and complete one side of

the poncho first (it does not matter which) before returning to work the other side.

The main pattern is an alternate pattern of chains of five flat knots. Beads are threaded onto and between chains as required, in the following arrangements: panels of beaded chains using single beads in each chain: tie two flat knots, slide a bead on to the knotbearing cords, tie another two flat knots to secure. Four panels of beaded arrangement are worked on each side of the poncho (see photograph opposite for arrangement). A centre beaded panel is worked for the front only; it includes the following arrangements of beads: work one knot, slide three beads on to the knotbearing cords, work another knot to secure. Pairs of beads are also threaded on to cords between the chains to give horizontal beading. Again refer to the photograph to see where the different beaded arrangements occur.

Continue until the poncho is the required length. Graduate the lower edge so it is deeper at the centre front and centre back by dropping a knot from each side on every row until the length is as required.

Work three rows of horizontal cording to finish.

TO FINISH

Trim the cord ends, leader cords and neck edge holding cords, and darn neatly into the back of the knotting.

Neck braid. Cut two cords, each 2 yd long, and set these on to a short holding cord. Introduce a separate leader about 3 yd long and work a braid of zig-zag cording long enough to fit round the neck edge of the poncho. When the braid is long enough trim the ends, join the two short ends of the braid together to form a circle, then stitch this in position to the neck edge of the poncho.

Outside edge braid. Work a similar braid to go right round the outside edge of the poncho; use three cords, each cut 12 yd long, and a leader of 14 yd. After each row of diagonal cording is worked, before the leader's direction is reversed to work the next row, slide a bead on to the leader cord. The braid should be about 180″ long when finished, to fit around the edge of the poncho. Join the short ends of the braid together, and then stitch the entire braid in position to the poncho edge.

Layette

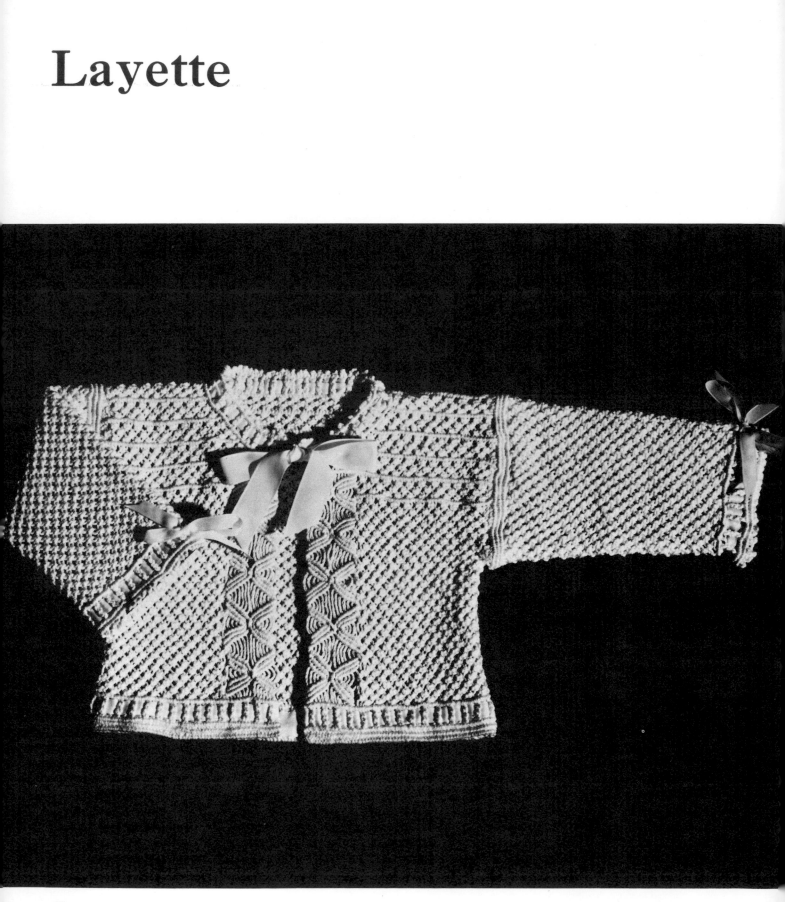

MATERIALS. For the jacket: 3 oz Wendy Invitation Cotton; 1 yd ribbon, $\frac{5}{8}''$ wide; 1 yd ribbon, $\frac{1}{4}''$ wide; $\frac{1}{2}$ yd seam binding, $\frac{5}{8}''$ wide.

For the shawl: quantity of yarn and ribbon depends on the finished size required, but 1 oz of Wendy Invitation Cotton will make a section about 8″ square, plus fringe. A length of ribbon, 1″ wide, will be required to thread through the outside edges.

MEASUREMENTS. The jacket will comfortably fit up to a 14″ chest size; length of jacket at centre back is 8″; sleeve seam is $5\frac{1}{2}''$.

TENSION CHECK. Chain of eight alternate half hitches measures $\frac{1}{2}''$.

PREPARATION FOR THE JACKET. The picot neck edging for the back and fronts of the jacket is worked first as a continuous strip. This is the only part of the jacket where curved shaping is required—the remainder of the jacket is worked straight. If possible, an existing jacket of similar size and shape should be used as a guide. Begin by cutting 59 cords, each 2 yd long. Set these on to a holding cord of about 15″ with overhand picot edging (see page 18). With each pair of cords work a single alternate half hitch chain to a depth of $\frac{5}{8}''$. Cut a separate leader, about 15″, and work a row of horizontal cording across all cords. Now unpin work from the board, and fold the strip so that the centre 4″ will form the back neck edge; the remaining ends will form the right and left front edges respectively. Gently pull the ends of the leader and holding cords to draw the front edges down into a curve—this is where a ready-made garment or paper pattern will be useful as a guide. When you are satisfied that the curve of the front neckline is right, trim the leader and holding cords to about an inch, press to the back of the work and secure with a few neat overcasting stitches. Alternatively, before trimming the ends, thread each end on to a large-eyed darning needle and darn into the back of the work.

Work now proceeds flat, working the front of the jacket first. Counting from the centre front, select the 10th alternate half hitch chain worked on the left front and the 16th alternate half hitch chain worked on the right front. These double cords form each shoulder edge, and the remaining cords for front and back are set on to them. For each front, cut 16 cords, each 2 yd long. Pin the worked neck edge to a working surface, so the shoulder cords are in position to use as holding cords, and set cords on to them.

TO MAKE THE JACKET

Left front. Working from the shoulder edge down, work three rows in alternate flat knot pattern, tying knots close together to give a dense fabric. On the 2nd row bring the next two cords from the neck edge into the pattern.

Next row: with the cord on the far left (coming from the neck edge) as leader, work a row of horizontal cording. Continue in this way working three-row bands of alternate flat knots, divided by rows of horizontal cording, gradually bringing the cords from the neck edge into the pattern until a row of flat knots is worked across all cords. Work another row of horizontal cording. Leave the first 16 cords unworked for the moment, and with the remaining cords work another three-row band of alternate flat knots, followed by a row of horizontal cording. Work now continues on these cords for another $4\frac{1}{4}''$ in the alternate flat knot pattern. On the first 16 cords, three-row crossovers of diagonal cording are worked to the same depth as the alternate flat knots. If wished, the flat knots and the cording motifs may be worked separately, and the edges where the two pattern strips meet will be stitched together later. Alternatively, the two bands of pattern may be worked concurrently and the end cords from one looped round the end cords of the other at regular intervals to link them together. Work the cording motif.

With cord 1 as leader slanting down to the right, work diagonal cording with cords 2, 3, 4, 5, 6, 7 and 8. Work a 2nd row below with cord 2 as leader, and knotting over it cords 3, 4, 5, 6, 7 and 8. Then work a 3rd row with cord 3 as leader, and knotting over it cords 4, 5, 6, 7 and 8.

With cord 16 as leader slanting down to the left, work diagonal cording with cords 15, 14, 13, 12, 11, 10 and 9. Work a 2nd row with cord 15 as leader, and knotting over it cords 14, 13, 12, 11, 10 and 9. Then work a 3rd row with cord 14 as leader, and knotting over it cords 13, 12, 11, 10 and 9.

Complete the lower half of the motif.

Reverse direction of cord 3 to form a leader slanting down to the left and work diagonal cording with cords 8, 7, 6, 5 and 4.

Reverse the direction of cord 2 to form a leader slanting down to the left and work diagonal cording over it with cords 8, 7, 6, 5, 4 and 3. Loop cord 1 round cord 16 then let cord 1 continue as leader for the 3rd row of diagonal cording and work over it with cords 8, 7, 6, 5, 4, 3 and 2. Complete the remaining section of the motif to match.

When motifs and flat knots have been completed, work a row of horizontal cording across.

Divide cords into pairs and work an alternate half hitch chain with each for $\frac{5}{8}''$.

Work three rows of cording to finish.

Right front. Work as for left front, reversing shaping so the cording motifs lie at the end of the row (for centre front edge) instead of at the beginning.

Back. When the fronts are completed, unpin the work and turn it round so the back neck edge is facing.

Layette

Cut **32** cords, each 2 yd long and set **16** on to each shoulder edge over those set on for the jacket fronts.

Work five bands of three rows of flat knots followed by a row of horizontal cording (as for the front yoke section) then continue in alternate flat knots until the back measures the same as the fronts, to the end of the flat knot section.

Complete the lower edge with chains of alternate half hitches and rows of horizontal cording, as for the fronts.

Sleeves (make 2 alike). Cut 42 cords, each 4 ft long. Set these on to a holding cord about 12″ long with overhand picot edging as for the jacket neck edge. With a separate leader (about 12″), work a row of horizontal cording.

Divide cords into pairs and work alternate half hitch chains to a depth of about ¼″. With a separate leader (about 12″), work a row of horizontal cording.

Now continue in the alternate flat knot pattern until the sleeve measures 5″ (or length required). Finish with three rows of horizontal cording.

TO FINISH JACKET

Stitch side seams. Stitch each sleeve seam, first trimming the ends of the holding and leader cords, then folding them to the inside of the work so they are sandwiched in the seam. Set each sleeve into each armhole by threading cords from the armhole edge of each sleeve individually on to a large-eyed darning needle, and sewing from the right through to the wrong side of the jacket in position along the armhole. Carefully darn ends into the back of the work, and trim ends when darning is complete.

Cut the narrow ribbon in half and thread a length through the alternate half hitch chains around each cuff edge.

Cut the wider ribbon in half, and thread one length through the neck edge half hitch chains to form a ribbon tie. Thread the other length through the half hitch chains at the hem edge. Turn each end of the ribbon at the centre front edges to the wrong side of the work. Trim cord ends at the lower edge to about an inch, then press them to the wrong side; stitch seam binding on the inside round the entire lower edge to enclose cord ends and ribbon.

PREPARATION FOR THE SHAWL.

Decide the width required for the central flat knot section of the shawl and set a number of cords on to a holding cord to give this measurement; (as a rough guide, four set-on cords on the holding cord measure 1″). Cut each cord to eight times the total length required (this measurement should include one complete fringe—the other one is added afterwards).

TO MAKE THE SHAWL

Work in the alternate flat knot pattern as for the jacket, to the required length.

Introduce a separate leader which should be long enough to go round all four sides of the shawl and work a row of horizontal cording.

Divide cords into pairs and work an alternate half hitch chain with each pair of cords to a depth of about 1″.

Introduce another separate leader, again long enough to go round all four sides of the shawl, and work a row of horizontal cording.

Now work the fringe as follows.

Divide cords into groups of 12. On the first group, leave the first cord unworked for the moment. With the next pair of cords tie two alternate half hitches; with the next pair, tie four alternate half hitches; with the next pair, tie six; with the next pair, four; with the next pair, two; and leave the last cord unworked. Now work a three-row V of cording: with cord 1 as leader slanting down to the right, work diagonal cording over it with cords 2, 3, 4, 5 and 6. With cord 12 as leader slanting down to the left, work diagonal cording over it with cords 11, 10, 9, 8 and 7. Link leaders at the tip of the V by knotting cord 12 over cord 1.

Work another two rows of diagonal cording immediately below this first one, using the outside cords as leaders for each row and linking the leaders in the centre each time.

When motifs have been worked across the row, work chains of alternate half hitches with pairs of cords between the motifs, graduating them as before: this means that between each pair of motifs you will work a four-knot chain, six-knot chain, eight-knot chain, six-knot chain and a four-knot chain, in that order.

Work another band of three-row cording Vs, alternating the sequence, i.e. each unit of twelve cords will comprise cords 7 to 12 and 1 to 6 from motifs of the previous cording band.

Tie each pair of cords with an overhand knot and trim the ends to give a fringe of the required depth.

TO FINISH THE SHAWL

Cut a number of cords, each 30″ long, and set these on all the way round the other three sides of the shawl.

Continuing with the leader from the first row of cording already worked, work horizontal cording round all cords.

Divide cords in pairs and work alternate half hitch chains as before.

Continuing with the leader from the second row of cording already worked, work horizontal cording round all cords.

Work the fringe to match the first section. If necessary set on more cords at the corners to fill in the fringe at these areas.

Tasselled cap

MATERIALS. Two 4 oz cones of Glacé for macramé by English Sewing Ltd.

MEASUREMENTS. To fit average-sized head; depth of cap from crown to outer edge 7″.

TENSION CHECK. Two flat knots measure $\frac{1}{4}$″.

PREPARATION. Cut 20 cords, each 40″ long. Place these cords together and make a tight binding round the whole bunch about 10″ from one end. Work now proceeds downwards from this point. As the cap is worked in the round, a suitable three-dimensional base will have to be used; a wig stand is ideal. Position the cords on your working base, so the tasselled top is at the highest point on your base. Spread the 20 working ends round evenly. New cords are cut and added as knotting progresses to give increased width to the cap; these will be described at the appropriate point in the design in the following instructions.

TO MAKE

The cap is worked in panels of different knotting patterns as follows.

1st panel: chains of two flat knots with each group of four cords.

Dividing row of horizontal cording (introduce a separate circular leader): 20 new cords are added here, each cut to 5 ft; four are added between each pair of flat knot chains. Total of 60 working ends.

Note. *Cords are doubled and set on the leader with double half hitches.*

2nd panel: single flat knots worked round on each group of four cords, then chains of three flat knots worked in the alternate sequence from the last row of knots. After the third knot in each chain is worked, add two extra cords, each 5 ft long, to give four extra working ends. The extra cords can be threaded round the loop of the last knot in each chain. Total of 120 working ends.

3rd panel: work in a single alternate flat knot pattern for two rows, then, maintaining the alternate pattern, work chains of two flat knots. Work two rows more of single alternate flat knots.

Still keeping to the alternate pattern, work single flat knots with every second group of four cords to the end of the round (leave the other cords unworked for the moment).

4th panel: work a criss-cross pattern of flat knot chains, tying each chain with two cords from the last row of flat knots and the two cords nearest to it left unworked in the previous row.

Tie two flat knots in each chain, then combine the pairs of chains together by tying a multi-end flat knot. At this point loop in two more new cords to each group, each new cord cut to 3 ft long. Divide into chains after the multi-end flat knot and complete each chain with two more flat knots. Tie a single flat knot below the multi-end knot with the four new cords. Total of 180 working ends.

Note. *No more new cords need now be added; to achieve any further shaping, slacken or tighten knots as required.*

If preferred, further new cords may in fact be looped in where appropriate.

Work single flat knots right round in an alternate sequence.

5th panel: still in the alternate pattern, work chains of two flat knots.

Work a single row of flat knots, continuing in alternate sequence.

6th panel: work double row crossovers of diagonal cording on each group of 12 cords right round. Link the crossover point on each motif by **knotting the right-hand leader over the left-hand leader.**

Tie a single flat knot to link the motifs together with the two outer cords from each motif.

7th panel: work in a single **alternate flat knot pattern,** but form 15 diamond panels of knots by stopping the knotting on each successive row (working in groups of 12 cords) two cords from each end until eventually a row is worked with only one flat knot in it.

8th panel: selecting leaders from the tip of each diamond, work cording down each side close to the last flat knots to form the top two sides of the diamonds.

Tie a multi-end flat knot with all the cords within each inverted V of cording just worked (three knotting cords from each side, four central knotbearing cords).

Link the leaders to each other all the way round, by always knotting the right-hand leader over the left-hand one.

Complete the lower two sides of each diamond by working diagonal cording over the same leaders.

Between each motif along the lower edge, divide the cords into groups of three, six and three.

Collect these groups by working several half hitches from the left with the cord on the far left in each group. Introduce a separate circular leader and work a row of horizontal cording round all cords.

Working on every second group of four cords right round, tie flat knot balls (see **page 76**). Leave the other cords unworked.

Finish with two rows of horizontal cording right round, immediately below the flat knot balls.

TO FINISH

Trim the ends, press to the inside of the cap and secure with a line of running stitches.

Work a coil knot at the tip of each cord on the crown tassel as follows: form a large loop near the end of the cord. At the point where the loop crosses, wind the cord round itself several times. Gently pull both ends of the cord and the 'winds' will form themselves into a coil. The more winds you work the deeper will be the coil produced.

Braid bag

Designed by Christine Hanscomb

MATERIALS. 177 yd Russia braid No. 4; two 10″ lengths of wooden dowelling; lining fabric (optional).

MEASUREMENTS. Maximum depth of bag to centre tip, excluding fringe, is 12″; width at widest point is 10″.

TENSION CHECK. One Josephine knot, tied with double strands, measures ¾″ across.

PREPARATION. Both sides of the bag are made alike. For each side therefore, cut 24 cords, each 3 yd long. Set these directly on to a length of dowelling.

TO MAKE

With the cord on the far left as leader, work a row of horizontal cording across all cords.

Reverse the direction of the leader and work a second row of horizontal cording from right to left across all cords.

Leave the first two cords unworked for the moment; tie a Josephine knot with each of the next five groups of four cords (using double thickness knotting cords).

Continuing to work on these cords only, work rows of Josephine knots (see page 30) in the alternate sequence, tying one knot fewer in each row (i.e. dropping two cords from each end of every row) until you reach the row with only one Josephine knot.

Continuing across the work, leave the centre four cords unworked, then work another panel of Josephine knots like the first on the next 20 cords. Leave the final two cords unworked.

Return to the cords at the beginning.

With cord 1 as a leader slanting down to the right, work diagonal cording over it with cord 2, then with all the cords coming from the left-hand side of the Josephine knot panel.

Continuing to use the cord on the far left as leader for each row, work 10 more rows of diagonal cording beneath the first. Stop cording on the same cord for every row (i.e. do not let the leader cords drop down to become knotting cords in subsequent rows).

In a similar way, work a six-row band of cording slanting down to left on the other side of the Josephine knot panel, and a six-row band of diagonal cording slanting down to the right on the left-hand side of the second Josephine knot panel. Cords from the centre will be used as leaders for these bands, and will cross from one side of the work to the other, so the inverted V panel of cording is linked in the centre.

Work 11 rows of cording slanting down to the left on the right-hand side of the second Josephine knot panel, using the cord at the far right as leader for every row.

At the tip of each Josephine knot panel, work a flat knot ball (see page 76), with the leaders from the last two rows of cording on each side. Tie four flat knots before taking the knotbearing cords up and over the chain.

In the centre of the inverted V of cording tie two multi-end flat knots, using single thickness knotting cords, and multiple knotbearing cords.

With the cord on the far left as leader, work a row of horizontal cording immediately below the edge of the previous panel of diagonal cording, using all the cords hanging from that edge to work the cording.

Work another three rows immediately below using the same leader for each row, and reversing its direction at the end of each row.

Now work another two rows of cording immediately below these four rows, using two left-hand cords from the flat knot balls as leaders. In each row work right along every cord to the end.

Work a similar panel of six-row cording with the cords at the far right of the work.

Complete the lower half of the central diamond of cording to match the upper half.

Now work two diamond panels of Josephine knots in alternate sequence, starting immediately below each flat knot ball. Begin with a single knot, and work one more knot in each row until the full width of the diamond is reached, then reduce by one knot in each row, as before. Work another central diamond of cording below the first, in a similar way.

At each side of the cording diamond, at a central point, work a flat knot ball.

Braid bag

TO FINISH

To make the handle, cut four cords, each eight times the required length of the finished handle. Set these directly on to one end of the dowelling on one side of the bag, over cords already set on; set the new threads on so they are hanging in the opposite direction from the main bag threads.

The handle pattern is worked in sections as follows: chains of flat knots with each group of four cords, with a flat knot ball in the centre of the chain. Then combine the cords and work a multi-end flat knot ball, followed by a strip of Josephine knots (four knotting cords from each side); then work another multi-end flat knot ball and divide the cords into two groups of four

Continue in this way and work chains of flat knots followed by Josephine knots, ending with chains of flat knots to match the chains worked at the beginning of the handle. The length worked of each section depends on the length of handle required.

When the handle is complete, loop the cord ends round the other end of the dowelling, take the cords to the back of the work and tie in a flat knot to secure. Trim ends.

Cut six more cords, each 10″ long. Set these on to the dowelling on which the handle was worked, position two cords exactly in the centre of the dowelling; then position two cords about ¾″ away on either side. Again set cords on so that they hang in the opposite direction from the main bag cords.

With each four cords, work a chain of flat knots to about 1″. Fold the chains back on themselves so the cord ends are on the wrong side of the work. Tie another flat knot to secure in this position. Stitch ends to the inside of the work to neaten.

Now place the two bag sections together, wrong sides facing, and oversew the sides together for about 4″ from each lower corner (leave the top unstitched so the bag can open freely).

Cut three more cords, each 8″ long. Set these on to the second dowelling rod with a simple picot edging (see page 18), positioning one opposite each flat knot ball on the first dowelling. Make the picot loops large enough to fasten comfortably over a flat knot ball.

Along the lower edge of the bag, tie the cords together in groups of four with overhand knots, combining two cords from each side of the bag in every knot to close the lower edge.

If wished, make a lining to fit the bag. Insert it into the bag, wrong sides facing; oversew round the inside of the top edge.

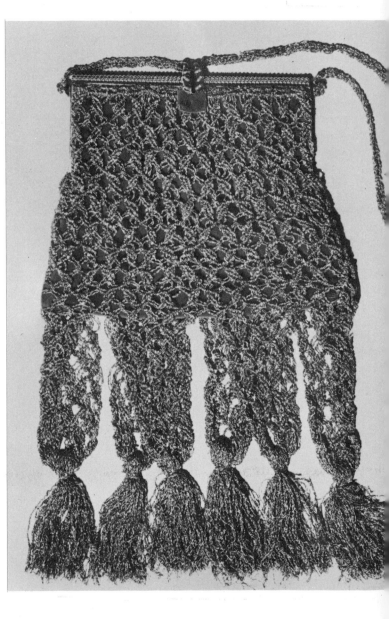

Evening bag

MATERIALS. Five balls of Jaeger Astral Spun; a 7″ bag frame; fabric and lining material to make up bag; jewelled clasp (optional).

MEASUREMENTS. The bag itself measures 7″ wide by 7″ long, but the macramé covering measures 11½″ long, excluding tassels.

TENSION CHECK. Each three-row cording motif measures ½″.

PREPARATION. Each side of the bag is made alike. For each side therefore cut 35 cords, each 3 yd long. Cut a holding cord approximately 1 ft long, and set cords on to this. Before beginning work it is advisable to dip the cord ends into colourless nail varnish to prevent them from unravelling.

TO MAKE

With the cord on the far left as leader, work 1 row of horizontal cording across all cords. Now begin pattern. Divide cords into groups of five.

With the first group, work three rows of diagonal cording slanting down to the left, using the cord on the far right as leader for each row. Each leader will drop down to become a knotting cord in subsequent rows.

With the second group of five cords, work three rows of diagonal cording slanting down to the right, using the cord on the far left as leader for each row.

Continue in this way across the row, working groups of diagonal cording alternately to the left and right.

Next row: between the first and second motifs of the previous row loop two right-hand cords from the first motif round two left-hand cords of the second motif.

Between the second and third motifs link the leaders by knotting the leader from the second motif over the leader of the third.

Continue in this way across the row, alternately looping cords together to link motifs, and knotting the leaders together.

Next row: work as for first row, but begin with three rows of cording slanting down to the right. Continue in this way until you have worked three bands of cording motifs altogether.

Now work the other side of the evening bag to the same point.

Work now proceeds in the round, so unpin work from your flat working surface, and use a suitable three-dimensional working base. Place the bag sections together, wrong sides facing.

At each lower corner tie together the outside cord from each side in a loose half knot. Set on over this half knot 10 new cords, each cut to 2 yd 1 ft. This will link the sides of the bag together. Repeat at the other lower corner, setting on 10 new cords in the same way.

Now continue in pattern, bringing new cords into the pattern, until another six bands of cording motifs have been worked.

Divide the cords into two groups of 25 on each side of the bag, and a group of 30 at each corner. Work in pattern on each group of cords separately until six bands of cording motifs have been worked from the point where the work divided.

TO FINISH

Trim the holding cord to 1″ at either end, turn to the wrong side and secure at the back of the work with a few overcasting stitches. Make a flat knot chain handle with four cords to the length required.

Make up the bag with fabric, lining and frame. Stitch macramé fabric in place to the right side of the bag, stitching round the top edges and down the sides as far as the bottom of the bag frame.

Stitch the handle in place.

Finish each long macramé strip with a 4″ tassel (see page 42 for instructions).

Add a clasp to fasten, if wished.

Shoulder bag

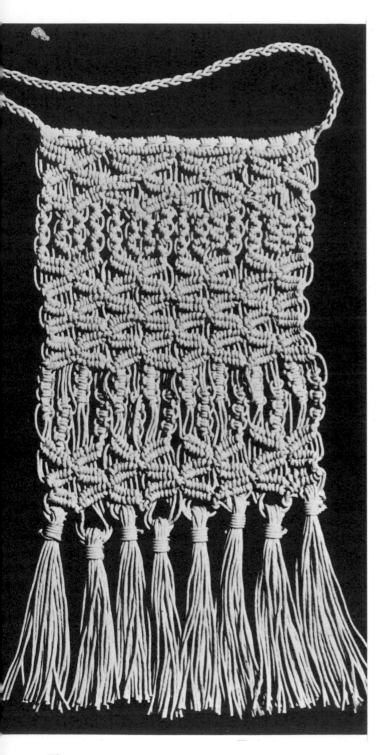

MATERIALS. 2 balls W. H. Smith C3 medium string; piece of lining fabric 15″ by 21″ (optional).

MEASUREMENTS. Bag measures 7″ wide, 10″ long, excluding tassels.

TENSION CHECK. Eight loops of cording measured on a horizontal row are 1″.

PREPARATION. For each side of the bag, cut 32 cords, each 80″ long. For the first side of the bag, cut a double thickness holding cord which should measure 10″, plus double the total measurement required for the bag handle (e.g. if you want a finished handle length of 20″, cut 50″ cord). Pin this double holding cord centrally to your working surface then set cords on in pairs. For the second side of the bag, cut a double thickness holding cord of about 16″ and set the remaining 32 cords on to this, also setting them on in pairs.

Note. *Throughout this design, cording, both horizontal and diagonal, is worked with a single loop on the leader cord, i.e. single half hitches, instead of double.*

TO MAKE

First side of bag. Cut a leader to the same measurement as the holding cord. Lay it centrally across the work, and work cording (single half hitches) over it with every cord to the end of the row.

Work double row crossovers of diagonal cording with each group of 16 cords to the end of the row. Link the central point of each crossover by knotting the left-hand leader over the right-hand leader.

Work another half band of this pattern, linking the tips of the motifs by knotting one leader over another.

Now divide the cords into groups of four, and work zig-zag chains of diagonal cording on each. The leader for every chain will be the cord on the far right. Work four zig-zags with the cords coming from the top of the previous motif, three zig-zags with cords coming from the bottom of the previous motif.

Work three more bands of double row crossovers of diagonal cording as before.

Divide cords into groups of four.

Work chains of reversed double half hitches with each group, using the outer cords as knotting cords, two central cords as knotbearers. Work six knots in each chain, but with the first and all odd-numbered chains work the six knots at the top of the cords, then leave an area of unworked cords below. With the second and all

Josephine belt

Designed by Christine Hanscomb

even-numbered cords, leave an unworked area of cords at the top, then work a chain of six knots starting around the point where the odd-numbered chains end.

Work 1½ bands of double row crossovers of diagonal cording as before.

Other side of bag. Work as for the first side, but cut the leader for the first row of horizontal cording to about 16″.

TO FINISH

On the first side of the bag, work a plaited handle at each side of the top edge, using the two strands from the holding cord and one from the leader cord to work the plait. When the plaits are the desired length tie the ends together with an overhand knot.

On the other side of the bag, trim the holding and leader cord ends to 1″, press to the wrong side of the work, and stitch neatly in place to the back of the work.

Place the bag sections together, wrong sides facing, and oversew neatly together down the side edges. Make 5″ tassels along the lower edge, as described on page 42, combining cords from the front and back of the bag in every tassel; this closes the lower edge.

If wished, make up a lining to fit the bag, insert into the bag and, with wrong sides together, sew it in place round the inside top edge.

MATERIALS. 50 ft of heavy cord.

MEASUREMENTS. To fit an average waist size 24/26″.

TENSION CHECK. One Josephine knot measures approximately 1½″ by 2½″.

PREPARATION. Cut yarn into four equal lengths, each 12 ft 6″ long.

TO MAKE

Place four cords side by side on your working surface. Starting about 27″ from one end (depending on how long you wish the ties to be) tie a chain of Josephine knots (see page 30), working them from the same direction every time, and keeping each knot close below the previous one. Tie 13 knots in all (or enough to fit the waist).

TO FINISH

Bind the ends of the cords tightly with cotton thread to prevent unravelling. If the first and last knots are inclined to slip, a tiny dab of fabric adhesive should keep them firmly in place.

Note. *Tying the Josephine knots from the same direction each time gives the belt a slight twist which makes it fit snugly to the curve of a waist. If it is preferred to have a straighter belt, alternate the direction in which each knot is worked.*

Rug

MATERIALS. Furnishing piping cord, $\frac{1}{2}''$ in diameter.

MEASUREMENTS. Variable; it can be any size wished.

TENSION CHECK. One flat knot measures 1″ across; two flat knots measure 1″ deep; two set-on cords on the holding cord measure 1″.

PREPARATION. Set a number of cords on a holding cord to measure the required width of the finished rug. Cut cords to eight times the finished measurement required, including a fringe at one end.

TO MAKE

Work two rows of alternate flat knot pattern.

Cords now divide into groups of 12 and four alternately across the row. Work groups of 12 cords in the alternate flat knot pattern. Work groups of four as chains of flat knots, but space out the knots at intervals on the knot-bearing cords.

When the work is the required length, work two rows straight across in the alternate flat knot pattern.

With separate leaders, work two rows of horizontal cording across all cords.

Lower border. Divide cords into groups of four and three at random. Work these groups in any knotted chain as wished: e.g. flat knot chains; half knot spirals; two flat knots, followed by a Josephine knot, followed by two flat knots; one flat knot, cross cord 2 over 1, and 4 over 3, another flat knot, followed by a third flat knot 1″ below; three-cord groups in reversed double half hitches worked continuously from the same side with one knotting cord over two knotbearers.

Work all the chains to a depth of 3½" (or as wished). Work another row of horizontal cording with a separate leader.

TO FINISH

Tie each group of four cords below the horizontal cording in single flat knots, then tie each individual cord in an overhand knot close to the flat knot just worked. Trim the cords to give a fringe of the required depth, and fray out ends if wished.

Now cut a number of cords equal to the number of set-on cords used for the rug, each about 8 ft long. Set these directly on to the set-on edge of the rug, over the cords already set on, but have them hanging in the opposite direction.

With separate leaders, work two rows of horizontal cording across these new cords, then divide cords into groups of four and three; work a border to match the one at the other end. Finish with a row of horizontal cording and a fringe, as before.

Trim the holding and leader cords to about an inch, press to the wrong side of the work, and secure them at the back with a few overcasting stitches.

Hammock

MATERIALS. 375 yd Strutt's piping cord No. 6; two lengths of wooden dowelling, each ⅞" in diameter and 20" long.

MEASUREMENTS. Finished hammock measures approximately 70" long, excluding fringe, and 27" wide at the widest point.

TENSION CHECK. Each flat knot measures 1¼" across, 1" deep.

PREPARATION. Cut 45 cords, each 25 ft long. Lay these single cords side by side (i.e. cords are not set on doubled as usual) on a working surface; as you are working on a large scale, a suitable area of floor is probably the most convenient working surface. Measure down from the cord ends the depth of fringe required, then from this point work two rows of the alternate flat knot pattern (as you have an unequal number of cords, one flat knot—preferably an end one—will use 5 cords, with three knotbearing cords).

Now lay one dowelling rod across the cords close to the last row of flat knots. Bring the central knotbearing cords of each knot over the top of the dowelling, leave the knotting cords under it. Now work a row of flat knots

below the dowelling, tying each knot fairly tightly to secure the dowelling.

TO MAKE

Continue in the alternate flat knots for another four rows. Work now proceeds with areas of unworked cords and single rows of five end flat knots (three knotbearing cords in each knot) divided by rows of horizontal cording.

Areas of unworked cords can be as deep as you wish, and cording rows can be curved to give shaping to the hammock. In order to increase the width of the hammock towards the centre, in the cording rows work three half hitches with each cord, instead of the normal two.

Finish with five rows of alternate flat knots to match the beginning of the hammock.

TO FINISH

Lay the other dowelling rod across cords; bring the knotbearing cords over the top of it, and the knotting cords under it, as before. Secure on the other side of the dowelling with two rows of flat knots in the alternate pattern.

Trim the fringe to match the one at the beginning. Fray out the ends if wished.

Lampshade

Shown on back cover

MATERIALS. 12 oz Twilley's dishcloth cotton; a drum lampshade, 10″ in diameter, 8″ deep; 4 yd binding tape.
MEASUREMENTS. To fit the lampshade frame.
TENSION CHECK. Three flat knots measure ½″.
PREPARATION. Bind the lampshade frame firmly with binding tape. The shade is worked in six panels: three panels of Pattern A, three panels of Pattern B, but with a slight variation for each panel. Panels may be worked separately then stitched at the side edges to the lampshade struts, or the entire shade may be worked continuously in the round. Whichever method you choose, it is best to set on all the cords at once to give a neat continuous top edge; cords may then be divided into groups and each panel worked separately if wished. For each panel (Pattern A or B), cut 28 threads, each 8 ft long. Set them directly on to the top edge of the frame, and work alternately with half hitch scalloped edging and overhand picot edging (see page 19) to give a decorative top edge.

76

TO MAKE
PATTERN A (make 3 times to form panels 1, 3 and 5)
With the cord on the far left as leader, work a row of horizontal cording.
1st pattern panel: divide cords into groups of four, and work chains of three flat knots with each group.
1st divider row: with the cord on the far right as leader, work a row of horizontal cording.
2nd pattern panel: divide cords into groups of four; work chains of half knots starting with 20 half knots in the left-hand spiral. Work one half knot fewer in each chain to the seventh (leave this seventh chain unworked for the moment), then increase each chain by one half knot on each of the remaining spirals to the right-hand chain. Let the spirals twist around themselves after every fourth knot.
To work the 7th chain: work two flat knots, then make a flat knot ball as follows. Work six more flat knots, leaving a small space between the first two flat knots in the chain and the six knots now being worked. After the sixth knot, bring the central knotbearing cords up in front of the chain, through to the back via the space above the chain, then pull them firmly down on the wrong side of the work. Tie another flat knot to secure the ball and hold it firmly in place. Work another two flat knots to complete the chain.
2nd divider row: with the cord on the far left as leader, work a row of cording across all cords, following the curved shaping created by the graduated spiral chains.
3rd pattern panel: work the alternate flat knot pattern for four rows from the top of the shaped curve (i.e. start at the highest point in the centre and gradually bring in the cords from either side as you work down).
Next row: keeping in pattern, work four knots from the left-hand side, then four knots from the right-hand side. Leave all the central cords unworked. Continuing on these sets of cords only, work another four rows in pattern, keeping the outside edges straight, but decreasing by one knot on each row at the inside edges to give a shaped central area.
Now with 36 cords in the centre, work one very big multi-end flat knot—have 10 knotting cords from each side, 16 knotbearing central cords.
With the 10 cords remaining at each side of the panel, continue working in the alternate flat knot pattern for seven rows (as you do not have a multiple of four in these

short rows, allow the extra cords to form loops at the ends of the rows where they occur).

Keeping in pattern, begin to increase on the inside shaped edges by bringing in two new cords to every row (at left and right) from the central cords coming from the multi-end flat knot.

Continue until the row is reached where flat knots are worked with every group of four cords right across the row.

3rd divider row: as first divider row.

4th pattern panel: as first pattern panel.

Turn work to the wrong side and work cording with every cord over the lower edge of the lampshade frame. Trim the ends to about 12".

PATTERN B (make one each of Versions 1, 2 and 3)

Version 1. Work first row of horizontal cording, first pattern panel and first divider row as for Pattern A.

2nd pattern panel: work spiral chains of 20 half knots with each group of four cords to the end, letting the spirals twist around themselves after every fourth knot.

2nd divider row: with the cord on the far left as leader work horizontal cording.

3rd pattern panel: work seven rows of a two-knot alternate flat knot pattern.

On the 7th chain of the 2nd row, work a flat knot ball as described for the 2nd pattern panel of Pattern A, but only tie four flat knots before taking the central cords up and over the chain.

In a similar way, tie flat knot balls on the 5th, 7th and 9th chains of the 4th row, and then on the 7th chain of the 6th row.

3rd divider row: as first divider row.

4th pattern panel: as 2nd pattern panel, but only tie 16 half knots in each spiral chain.

4th divider row: as 2nd divider row.

5th pattern panel: as first pattern panel.

Finish as for Pattern A, by working cording over the lampshade on the wrong side.

Version 2. Work as for Version 1, but in the 3rd pattern panel work flat knot balls as follows: on the 4th, 7th and 10th chains of the 2nd row; on the 5th, 8th and 11th chains of the 3rd row; on the 5th, 8th and 11th chains of the 4th row; on the 6th, 9th and 12th chains of the 5th row; and on the 6th, 9th and 12th chains of the 6th row. Complete as for Version 1.

Version 3. Work as for Version 1; but in the 3rd pattern panel work flat knot balls as follows: on the 1st, 3rd, 5th, 7th, 9th, 11th and 13th chains of the 4th row. Complete as for Version 1.

TO FINISH

To cover each side strut of the frame, cut three cords, each 8 ft long. Set these on to the top row of cording immediately above a side strut. Work a continuous flat knot chain for the length of the strut; use single knotting cords, four central knotbearing cords. At the end of the strut, take the cords to the wrong side of the frame and tie a flat knot on the wrong side over the strut. Trim the ends to about an inch, fold back on to the inside of the strut and secure with a few neat overcasting stitches.

If the shade has been worked continuously in the round, it is advisable to secure the knotted fabric to the side struts with a few neat stitches at occasional points—on cording divider rows, for instance.

Work two rows of the alternate flat knot pattern around the lower edge, using six cords for each knot (single knotting cords, four central knotbearing cords). Trim a fringe to the depth required and fray out the ends, if wished.

Tablemat

MATERIALS. 59 yd 1 ft of hemp (or any coarse, heavy string).

MEASUREMENTS. Mat measures 11″ by 9″.

TENSION CHECK. Three rows of flat knots over the alternate pattern measure 1″.

PREPARATION. Cut 20 cords, each 8 ft long; cut two cords, each 9 ft long. Pin one of the 9 ft lengths centrally to your working surface so it can be used as a holding cord. Set on the 20 cords to it with double half hitches, so the set-on edge resembles a row of cording. The ends of the holding cord now drop down to become knotting cords.

TO MAKE

Using the remaining 9 ft cord as leader, lay it centrally across the work, and work horizontal cording over it with all the cords to the end of the row. The ends of the leader cord now drop down to become knotting cords: total of 44 working ends.

Work in the alternate flat knot pattern for four rows.

Now divide for the central cording diamonds.

Work flat knots with each of the first three groups of four cords. Continue on these cords only, keeping in pattern, but working one knot fewer in each row on the right-hand edge until you work a row of only one flat knot.

Work a similar triangle of flat knots with 12 cords at the end of the row, but reduce the knots along the left-hand edge.

On the centre 12 cords, work a row of three flat knots, then a row of two, finally a row of one, dropping two cords from each end of every row.

Now work cording diamonds.

Numbering four unworked cords on the left of the central flat knot triangle from 1 to 4, use cord 2 as the first leader slanting down to the right, and work diagonal cording over it with cords 3 and 4, and all the cords coming from the left-hand side of the central flat knot triangle.

Work a 2nd row of cording immediately below, with cord 1 as leader.

Now work the left-hand side of the diamond; use cord 3 as leader for the first row, slanting down to the left, and work diagonal cording over it with all the cords from the sloped flat knot edge on that side.

Work a 2nd row of cording with cord 4 as leader. In a similar way work the top two sides of the second diamond. Link the diamonds together where the leaders cross by knotting cords 2 and 1 of the first diamond over cord 3 of the second diamond, and then over cord 4 of the second diamond.

Work a multi-end flat knot in the centre of each diamond, using four knotting cords from each side, and four central knotbearing core cords.

Let cords 3 and 4 from the second diamond continue across the work to form leaders slanting down to the left for the lower right-hand side of the first diamond. Work cording over each leader in turn with the six cords along that side. In a similar way let cords 2 and 1 from the first diamond continue across the work as leaders for the left-hand lower side of the second diamond. Work cording over each in turn with the six cords along that side.

Now work the remaining side for each diamond. Leaders for the first diamond will be the last two cords used to work cording over cords 3 and 4. Leaders for the second diamond will be the two cords coming from the flat knot nearest to the point where the cording is to begin. Cords 2 and 1 (used previously as leaders) will both now become knotting cords and will begin rows of cording by knotting over the new leaders. Link lower points of the diamonds by knotting the right-hand leaders over left-hand leaders.

Now tie another multi-end flat knot in the centre of the work, then let each set of leaders continue across the work to complete a centre (third) diamond.

Return to the cords at each side and fill in a triangle of flat knots at each side of the work.

From the point where flat knots stopped before, work rows increasing by one knot on each row on the inside edge until the point of the cording diamond is reached, then work another similar number of rows, reducing by one knot each time on the same edge until you work the row with only one knot in it. Complete the remaining two diamonds to match the others.

Continue in alternate flat knot pattern, first filling in the triangular areas around the last two cording diamonds, then working straight for four rows.

Finally, with the cord on the far left as leader, work two rows of horizontal cording, reversing the direction of the leader at the end of the first row, and working the 2nd row from right to left.

TO FINISH

Trim cords to about 1″, then weave the ends into the back of the knotting.

Cavandoli castle cushion

MATERIALS. 4 oz in each of 2 constrasting colours of F.A. dishcloth cotton. (1 lb drums of cotton can be ordered from the Handicraft Centre, P.O. Box 135, 37 Lever Street, Manchester M60 1UX); fabric cushion cover approximately $12\frac{1}{2}''$ by $15''$ in a colour to match or contrast with the colours of dishcloth cotton; a cushion pad approximately $12\frac{1}{2}''$ by $15''$.

MEASUREMENTS. Finished cushion measures approximately $12\frac{1}{2}''$ by $15''$.

TENSION CHECK. Six double loops on holding cord measure $1''$.

PREPARATION. Cut 70 threads in colour A (background colour), each 4 yd long. Set these on in pairs to a holding cord in colour A, about $20''$ long.

Note. *Cords are worked double throughout, so you now have 70 working ends.*

TO MAKE

Introduce a double thickness leader in colour B, and work in solid horizontal and vertical cording from the chart below. The leader may either be kept as a ball of yarn (remember to wind the ball so you have a double thickness of yarn to use) or may be cut into more manageable lengths, so new lengths can be introduced when required. In this case it is preferable to introduce the new lengths always at the beginning of a new row.

TO FINISH

Trim cord ends, and leader and holding cord ends to about $1''$. Press them to the back of the work and secure with a few neat stitches.

Stitch macramé fabric to one side of the cushion cover.

Note. *This design could be used as a central motif for a bedspread or a sweater.*

☐ Horizontal cording, colour A.
● Vertical cording, colour B.